THE TREASURES OF
ENGLISH CHURCHES

National Churches Trust

*For people who love
church buildings*

THE TREASURES OF ENGLISH CHURCHES

WITNESSES TO THE HISTORY OF A NATION

MATTHEW BYRNE

Supported by the National Churches Trust

SHIRE PUBLICATIONS

Bloomsbury Publishing Plc
Kemp House, Chawley Park, Cumnor Hill, Oxford OX2 9PH, UK
29 Earlsfort Terrace, Dublin 2, Ireland
1385 Broadway, 5th Floor, New York, NY 10018, USA

E-mail: shire@bloomsbury.com
www.shirebooks.co.uk

SHIRE is a trademark of Osprey Publishing

First published in Great Britain in 2021

A catalogue record for this book is available from the British Library.

ISBN: HB 978 1 78442 489 3; eBook 978 1 78442 488 6; ePDF 978 1 78442 487 9; XML 978 1 78442 490 9

21 22 23 24 25   10 9 8 7 6 5 4 3 2

Index by Zoe Ross
Typeset by Myriam Bell Design, UK
Printed and bound by Bell & Bain Ltd., Glasgow G46 7UQ

Shire Publications supports the Woodland Trust, the UK's leading woodland conservation charity.

Front cover: Hereford Cathedral. Sir Peter de Grandisson, d.1352. In the centre of the canopied figures Christ crowns his
mother Mary as Queen of Heaven.

Half-title: See page 115.

Title page: Lichfield Cathedral. Monument to the two young Robinson sisters who died of scarlet fever in 1812.

Page viii and back cover: Chancel ceiling of the Abbey Church of St Mary, Tewkesbury, Gloucestershire. The chancel was
rebuilt in the early fourteenth century by the noble de Clare and Despenser families. Its colourful ceiling is a complex
multi-ribbed (lierne) vault.

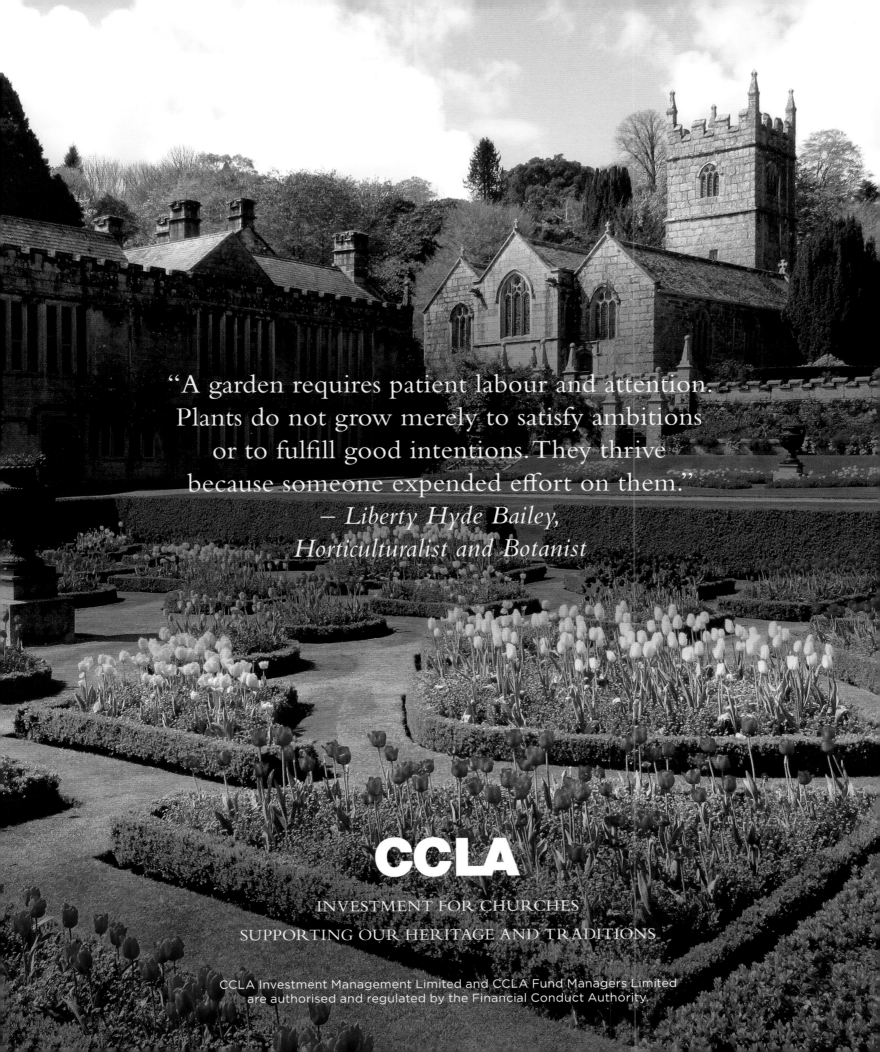

"A garden requires patient labour and attention. Plants do not grow merely to satisfy ambitions or to fulfill good intentions. They thrive because someone expended effort on them."
– *Liberty Hyde Bailey,*
Horticulturalist and Botanist

CCLA

INVESTMENT FOR CHURCHES

SUPPORTING OUR HERITAGE AND TRADITIONS

CONTENTS

KENSINGTON PALACE
LONDON W8 4PU

   Our churches are both a focal point and a symbol of the communities in which they are situated. As time has passed, they have accumulated further symbols of both national and local history.

   This book is a guide to those who like to explore the churches in places they may not already know, but would see their churches as a wonderful variety of historic realities that can be a great pleasure to those who can visit them.

   I hope that everyone who reads this book will share Matthew's love of this wonderful inheritance that we can all feel part of.

PREFACE

The National Churches Trust

Churches have been part of local and national landscapes for so many centuries that their presence is often taken for granted. However, ensuring that they remain safeguarded for the future is down to the hard work and dedication of local people and the provision of funding and support. The National Churches Trust and its predecessor charity, the Historic Churches Preservation Trust, are proud to have played a part in keeping churches alive since 1953.

Luke March, Chairman, National Churches Trust

THE NATIONAL CHURCHES TRUST IS the national, independent charity dedicated to the repair and support of the UK's churches, chapels and meeting houses. The Trust was created in 2007 to take forward the work of the Historic Churches Preservation Trust, founded in 1953. It does not own any buildings but rather supports those responsible for the upkeep of places of worship.

The Trust has helped virtually every church named in Simon Jenkins's *England's Thousand Best Churches*. Geographically, churches in all four corners of the British Isles have been covered by grants; from St Lawrence, Jersey, to St Magnus, Lerwick in Shetland, from Christ Church, Lowestoft in Suffolk, to St James, Moy in County Tyrone.

In 2020, the Trust awarded or recommended over 220 grants worth more than £1.6 million – funding that was much needed as many churches faced severe funding shortages during the Covid-19 pandemic.

The National Churches Trust's key areas of work include:

1. Keeping churches at the heart of communities in the UK's cities, towns and villages. Many are under threat from leaking roofs, crumbling stonework and rotting timbers. We want to make sure that their architecture and history are there for future generations to enjoy. The Trust does this by providing grants for the repair, restoration and maintenance of church buildings, and by supporting projects that enable churches to be at the centre of local communities through the provision of modern facilities such as toilets, kitchens and improving access. Since 2007, we have funded over 2,000 projects at churches, chapels and meeting houses throughout the UK with grants totalling over £20 million.

2. Encouraging regular maintenance of church buildings by providing practical advice, support and information. Maintenance preserves heritage, saves money, energy and materials, prevents large repair bills and promotes good guardianship and community involvement. The website

The church of St Mary the Virgin in Alton Barnes, Wiltshire, is one of the smallest in England. A project to help fund a major restoration project, including repairs to the roof and dealing with damp in the walls and timberwork, is one of over 2,000 projects the National Churches Trust has funded since 2007. © Manor Studios

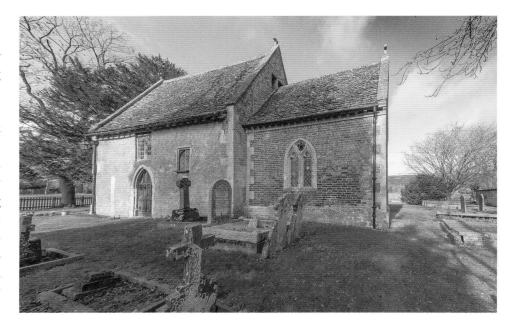

MaintenanceBooker (www.maintenancebooker. org.uk) makes it easy for churches, chapels and meeting houses to book maintenance services with accredited and experienced contractors.

3. Promoting church tourism and bringing a new generation of people into contact with church history and architecture. ExploreChurches (www.explorechurches.org) makes it easy to discover the UK's magnificent sacred heritage. The website includes full information about some of the UK's best loved churches together with opening times, travel information and how to make the most of visiting churches. Getting more

people to value our shared heritage of church buildings is a great way of ensuring their long-term sustainability.

4. Working to increase awareness among the public and decision makers of the value of places of worship. As well as being places of worship, church buildings play an important role in helping local people. It is estimated that nearly 90% of churches are used for community purposes. In 2020 the Trust published a pioneering economic study that measured the extent of the social and economic value that the UK's 40,300 church buildings provide to the nation and local communities. It examined church buildings open to the public and being used for Christian worship. In the UK, the total social value of church buildings calculated so far is at least £12.4 billion annually: roughly equal to the total NHS spending in England on mental health in 2018.

The National Churches Trust receives no income from either government or church authorities and relies on Friends and supporters to continue its work. You can find information about how to support the Trust by visiting:

www.nationalchurchestrust.org/support

Above: Keeping the UK's priceless heritage of church buildings windproof and watertight is at the heart of the work of the National Churches Trust, as shown by roof repairs at St-Just-in-Penwith, St Just, Penzance, Cornwall. © David Osborne-Broad

Right: Discovering St Mary's church in Horncastle, Lincolnshire, one of over 3,000 churches, chapels and meeting houses featured on the National Churches Trust's ExploreChurches website. © ExploreChurches

The 'Mynstrells' at St Mary's Church, Beverley, East Yorkshire. The jolly, heart-warming group is shown on a capital in the nave to mark their donation to its rebuilding in 1520.

INTRODUCTION

The Enduring Appeal of English Churches

One of the pleasures of English churches is the way in which they allow people to relate emotionally to their ancestors. The little Anglo-Saxon church at Escomb, County Durham, has hardly been altered since it was built in the eighth century and is still in regular use.

ENGLISH PARISH CHURCHES AND CATHEDRALS continue to attract the interest and affection of a wide range of people, as they always have. In 2018 there were over 10 million visitors to our cathedrals and many more to parish churches. This figure includes those who attend services on a regular basis as well as the great numbers of others who visit outside of services. The latter category covers both those who come on occasion as the opportunity arises and those for whom exploring these buildings regularly is a lifelong interest and joy.

In the twentieth century, nobody more exemplified the latter than poet laureate Sir John Betjeman (1906–1984), who wrote about English cathedrals and parish churches in innumerable essays, poems and books. His *Passion for Churches* (the title of a television series made in later life) was expressed eloquently and movingly in both serious and humorous vein: 'What would you be, you wide East Anglian sky, / Without church towers to recognise you by?' As an architectural historian he was able to write of the origins and character of ancient and modern churches, but he could never separate these things from stories of the individuals for whom the buildings were a central part of life: rectors, vicars, curates and laypeople. As a churchman – and sometime churchwarden – too, he had many opportunities to observe and record their commitment, weaknesses, eccentricities and foibles with warmth and understanding. The centuries-old link between buildings and people is a recurrent theme also in this book.

The origins of churches in England go back to the fourth century, in the later years of the Roman occupation of Britain, and they have been a prominent feature of the English landscape since the Anglo-Saxons began to accept Christianity in the seventh century. England is one of the few places in the world that has a group of buildings which for so many centuries has served without break the purpose for which they were built: preaching of the Christian gospel, celebration of the sacraments and as centres of service to their communities. Today these churches stand in vibrant city centres and their suburbs, in market towns, old industrial towns, in villages and hamlets and sometimes quite alone in hills and fields where the settlements they ministered to have long since disappeared. Until recently they would almost always have been the largest and tallest buildings in these places. Only in the twentieth century did churches start to be overshadowed by commercial and residential

English churches contain works of art that vary greatly in age and level of craftsmanship. They are particularly instructive when two refer to the same subject matter. These images of Christ are separated by 1,000 years but both succeed in capturing His character and mood in very different contexts.
Left: Coventry Cathedral's *Ecce Homo* (Behold The Man) by Jacob Epstein, 1934, depicts Christ being shown to the people by Pilate after His scourging and prior to His crucifixion. The work captures His implacable expression when, although bound with rope and tortured, He will not be deflected from His purpose.
Right: Barnack, Northamptonshire. *Christ in Majesty*, a wall-mounted Saxon sculpture, *c.*950. His suffering and earthly life complete, Christ now reigns for eternity on a throne in heaven. This piece is of 'exquisite quality, with an expression that is human, dignified and gentle'.

skyscrapers in many cities. But archaeology apart, they remain some of the most ancient evidence of humans' occupation of these lands.

What then is the appeal of churches? Apart from their size and age they include examples of the greatest architecture of the land alongside innumerable smaller, humble buildings as lovable as any architectural showpiece. More importantly for this book, within them are furnishings often as old as the buildings themselves, the monuments, sculpture sacred and secular, stained glass, the woodwork in roofs, screens, benches and pulpits as well as the occasional survival of all manner of curiosities, relics of past customs.

However, English churches are more than a collection of art objects – no matter how impressive, beautiful or valuable these may be. Churches are meeting places between the Divine spirit and human beings, and the buildings and their furniture mirror human nature in all its aspects: piety and generosity on the one hand; pride, vanity and ambition on the other. Their current appearance results from changing attitudes in many spheres: religious, political, social, emotional and artistic. A knowledge of why, how and when these invisible factors created the visible legacies we have today is important in understanding, and hence enjoying, the exploration of a church. The marriage of photographs and text presented in this book is intended to help foster that enjoyment. I hope that it will also help encourage readers to venture out and discover for themselves England's wonderful churches.

Getting more people to visit churches is one way in which these magnificent buildings can be safeguarded for the future, as it helps to show those responsible for funding church buildings that they remain an important and loved part of our heritage.

CHURCH TREASURES: THEIR MANY ASPECTS AND PLEASURES

The word 'treasures' in the sense with which it is employed throughout this book has a wider meaning here than is often used in the world of art connoisseurs, as the preceding paragraphs have already implied.

Links with Past Generations

One value of an ancient building still in use for the purpose its builders intended is the way in which it connects us with the people of the past. Moreover, there are some church-lovers who feel a special empathy with people of a particular period. For some it is the Victorians, who built some 6,000 churches in sixty years. For others it is the Georgians and their classical tastes, which were so very different from the generations immediately before and after them. But for many who travel widely in search of our remoter churches, there is no greater emotion than when, in some small village off the beaten track, they see a small wooden fingerpost directing down a side-lane 'To The Saxon Church'. A church that pre-dates the Norman Conquest of 1066 is relatively rare and draws us back to the origins of England as a nation. The simple little

Two pulpits serving the same purpose but again of very different craftsmanship.
Left: City of London. St James Garlickhythe is one of Christopher Wren's churches of 1682. The contemporary carving is in the richly ornamental Baroque style.
Right: Lead, West Yorkshire. An early eighteenth-century two-decker pulpit by a local joiner.

The stained glass that has been a prominent feature of churches for 800 years is a mixture of the good, the bad and the indifferent. Two examples of the best are in sharp contrast but share richly glowing colours.
Left: Enville, Staffordshire. A Madonna and Child, c.1330. The beautiful borders are typical of medieval designs.
Right: Chichester Cathedral. By Marc Chagall, 1977, based on Psalm 150 'Praise Ye The Lord'. King David and other people play instruments mentioned in the psalm.

church at Escomb, County Durham, still in regular use, is an almost unaltered survival of the eighth century – although it actually embodies in part the stonework recovered from a nearby Roman villa. Such is the continuity of English building history, and for those who are sensitive to it there is as much pleasure to be had in such places as there is in their grandest successors of the later Middle Ages.

Fine Art and Craftsmanship

When Sir Christopher Wren (1632–1723) rebuilt the churches of the City of London after the Great Fire of 1666, he employed the finest woodcarvers in England and from abroad at a time when their craft had reached a pinnacle of excellence. Most notable among the craftsmen were the great Grinling Gibbons (1648–1721) and those working in his studio. Their screens, pulpits, reredoses, fonts, galleries, doorways and pews are adorned with garlands, cherubs, statuettes and abstract forms all so deeply and intricately undercut that they are almost three dimensional. There are some examples of this Baroque period in the London boroughs, Oxford and elsewhere.

The most prominent features in many English churches are the monuments, which vary in size from those that soar from floor to ceiling to small wall tablets. The former commemorate the great and the good – and the not so good – from the highest and wealthiest ranks of English society. The medieval period provides many such examples, but it is the seventeenth and eighteenth centuries that offer the most flamboyantly spectacular – from a time when dukes, earls, marquesses and other nobility employed the leading sculptors from home and abroad to carve their images, alone or as family groups, in gleaming white marble. These are masterpieces of theatre if not of Christian piety. Succeeding generations of a family might fill an entire church with these monuments. The fact that these churches are often quite humble buildings in quiet, secret places close to the ancestral homes where they wished to be remembered adds to the powerful experience of wandering among them – an awe made greater by the supreme skill of the sculptors. Many other examples of fine art will be found in the following pages.

Rustic Craftsmen Portraying Humble People

The woodcarving of Grinling Gibbons and his contemporaries in the City of London churches is certainly a wonder to behold, but by contrast in the quiet village of Ripple in Worcestershire the chancel of the parish church has a set of fifteenth-century stalls from the time that the area was served by a college of priests. The misericords (the undersides of the tip-up seats) have a series of twelve carvings by an unknown local craftsman, which portrays the lives of peasants in a rural village from January to December. These delightful

People who worshipped in churches have left visual reminders of themselves in various ways. Those of higher and lower status who paid for the large medieval stained-glass windows arranged for small 'donor panels' recording their generosity to be inserted at the bases. These two are both fifteenth century.
Left: St Neot, Cornwall. This, one of many in the church, shows members of the Martyn family. The Latin inscription below records their donation, while in the streamers above the men ask for the prayers of St John and the women those of St Stephen.
Right: Long Melford, Suffolk. Elizabeth, Duchess of Norfolk faces Elizabeth, Countess of Surrey. The Duchess may have been the model for John Tenniel's illustration of the duchess in Lewis Carroll's *Alice in Wonderland*.

Some churches possess memorabilia from previous generations. This nineteenth-century glass-sided hand-pulled hearse is at Evesham, Worcestershire.

cameos show men and women carrying out seasonal farming chores outdoors and indoors with their animals and crops. This work is not great art but the carvings are both 'delightfully lively' and fascinating, as we seem to be in close contact with the people of the parish some five hundred years ago (see Chapter 7).

There are many similar instances of contrast. For example, whilst we have the portraits of the wealthy and powerful in their monuments, along the wall of the north aisle in the fourteenth-century Beverley Minster in East Yorkshire a local stonemason has also carved a long line of rustic musicians playing a variety of stringed, wind and percussion instruments, forerunners of those in use today. They provide another fascinating glimpse of local men who may have performed in the church six hundred years ago (see Chapter 4).

Revealing Past Social and Religious Attitudes

When Henry VIII declared himself Head of the Church in England in 1531 and began to separate the country from the authority of the pope in Rome, this resulted in a number of changes in the ordering of church interiors. These increased in scope as his successor Edward VI led the Church farther away from its Catholic roots to a more Protestant theology and ritual. The eighteenth century brought yet more change.

Class distinctions had existed in all periods between the nobility and those below them, but in the eighteenth century these became more clearly defined between and within the middle and lower classes in all aspects of everyday life. This included worship in churches and the arrangements made to seat people now reflected gradations of status. In the mid-nineteenth century, parts of the Victorian Church shifted back towards a more 'Catholic' theology and liturgy. At the same time there was widespread rejection of blatant class distinctions inside churches and as a result whole interiors were swept away and replaced by those similar to what we have now (in some cases, these Victorian changes were funded by the Incorporated Church Building Society, a forerunner of the National Churches Trust). In some remote places, however, owing to conservatism or lack of funds, the old interiors remained untouched. Today visitors can enter these 'unrestored' churches and be immersed in an atmosphere in which Jane Austen and her characters would be completely at home. So, along with many other things, churches offer a way to understand social and religious history (see Chapter 15 for more on this aspect).

THE CHOICE OF CONTENTS: INCLUSIONS AND EXCLUSIONS

There have been many books on church treasures – some general, some confined to one feature. Thus there have been entire volumes on church monuments and stained glass, both of which are very large subjects. Even relatively smaller features such as Anglo-Saxon crosses, medieval carved bench ends, rood screens, monumental brasses, wall paintings and fonts have filled whole books. This book, which attempts a less specialised, more broadly representative coverage for the general reader, must of necessity, therefore, omit some features altogether and include others in a highly selective way. Rather than attempt wide-ranging outline surveys of whole fields such as stained glass, monuments or woodwork, specific examples within each area have been chosen to represent the whole. An important working principle has been that a significant number of chapters should be devoted to the many people, humble as well as grand, who have used English churches over the past 1,000 years. So their history as well as that of art and architecture is very much part of the story.

Another factor has limited the number of items that could be included. A photographer-author who wishes to do justice to the beauty of these subjects will require the photographs, which are the essence of the book, to be reproduced at the largest possible size and this places further constraint on the space available. A modern restaurateur might describe this book as the equivalent of one of their 'tasting menus'.

Church treasures are generally taken to be features inside the buildings, rather than the buildings themselves; accordingly, there is no description here of the history and architecture of churches as such (the author has covered those elements in three previous books). Nevertheless, an account that gave no sight of anything exterior would be lacking. The explorations of village churches will thus inevitably start in their churchyards, generally places of tranquillity, havens for wildlife and records of village history – all in the shadow of a venerable building. This combination makes a village churchyard a treasure for its community. As an example, the unique Cotswold village of Painswick provides an opportunity to explore a church within its surrounding context (Chapter 14).

There are some treasures of English churches that this book cannot show: the varied and often awe-inspiring situations and landscapes in which they are found. Exploring churches provides a great opportunity to travel: from the vibrant hearts of great cities to historical market towns, to the 'chocolate box' prettiness of Cotswold and West Country villages or the rugged beauty of the Lake District. In Cornwall, a county of sturdy granite churches, there is one that stands alone among sand dunes on an isolated beach and several within yards of cliff edges overlooking the Atlantic.

Those who have explored English churches have explored England, its landscapes, art, architecture and the history of its people.

IN CONCLUSION

The magnificent abbey church at Tewkesbury in Gloucestershire is an historical panorama of fine architecture, from the Norman period to the late medieval. It has an extensive collection of the finest stained glass, monuments, chantry chapels and other treasures of the highest order. However, there is a notice in the porch which reads: 'The treasures of this church are the gospel which it exists to proclaim, the traditions which it enshrines and the prayers and devotions of those who worship and serve here.' There are many things of great beauty in ancient and modern English churches, objects that museums and art galleries would willingly possess but which in these sacred places can be seen and used for the unchanging purposes that the abbey describes.

QUOTATIONS

Unless otherwise stated, all direct quotations are taken from the books of Nikolaus Pevsner (see Acknowledgements and Further Reading)

CHURCH DEDICATIONS

These are only included when there is more than one church in a given place.

8

1

THE ART OF THE EARLY ENGLISH CHURCH

Anglo-Saxon Sculpture 700–1066

Opposite: The Bewcastle
Cross of c.700–750 stands in
a remote hamlet in the wide,
rolling hills of the Cumbrian
border country. 'There is
nothing as perfect as this of
a comparable date in Europe.'
The west face shows three
figures in recesses. From top
to bottom: St John the Baptist
with an Agnus Dei; Christ;
St John the Evangelist – 'All
wonderfully calm, classically
dressed and posed.' The east
face has a single great vine
scroll inhabited by birds
and beasts.

WHEN EMPEROR CONSTANTINE LEGALISED THE Christian religion in the Roman Empire in 313, which later he made the official religion, the Romans had been in occupation of Britain for nearly 300 years. From 313 until the withdrawal of the Roman troops in 409, an infant church was born among peoples who consisted of Roman families, the native Celts who had been conquered and those born of intermarriage of the two. This early church has left us some physical evidence of itself (Chapter 6) but it did not survive the departure of the Roman establishment. This was followed by the arrival of invading Angles, Saxons and Jutes from northern Europe, resulting in a migration of the Celtic and Romano-Celtic people to the western fringes of Britain.

The reintroduction of Christianity came from two separate groups, who entered Britain from two opposite corners. In the fourth and fifth centuries, during the latter days of the Roman occupation, missionaries from Gaul (modern France) and western Britain had established a thriving Christian church in Ireland. In 563, St Columba and a group of monks travelled from north-east Ireland to found a monastery on the island of Iona off the west coast of Scotland. From here they and their successors journeyed to the Scottish mainland and then to an increasingly large area of northern England, converting a significant number of Anglo-Saxons in the kingdom of Northumbria. Then in 595, Pope Gregory in Rome sent a group of monks led by

St Augustine to evangelise the pagan Anglo-Saxons in southern England, where they arrived in Kent in 597. From these two places Christianity spread gradually over the following centuries, with periods of success and failure in a country divided between different kings who were frequently at war with one another and that suffered invasions of Vikings from the Scandinavian countries. Nevertheless, England became an essentially united and Christian country by the tenth century.

Looking at the art and architecture of the period, we therefore see a wide range of influences from the cultures of the Celts, the Roman Empire, the Anglo-Saxons and the Vikings. The Celts had originated in the Iron Age of the fifth century BC in Central Europe, from where they migrated to modern-day France, Britain and Ireland. From the first century AD they developed highly sophisticated forms of art in metalwork, jewellery, stonework and their famous illustrated manuscripts, all of which in turn show influence from Byzantine, Early Christian, Greek and even oriental sources. Augustine and his successors then brought the art and architecture of classical antiquity in an early form of Romanesque. So, the English Anglo-Saxons were influenced by both Celtic and Roman art, to which they added their own distinctive elements. Apart from illuminated manuscripts and some jewellery, the surviving religious art of this period is in the form of stone sculpture which can conveniently be considered under three headings: standing outdoor crosses, interior sculpture and free-standing furniture.

STANDING CROSSES

Celtic Christianity in Ireland and England, especially the former, is characterised by monolithic carved stone crosses placed originally in small settlements or in open country. They often now stand in the precincts of later churches – locations that may have been the crossing points of trackways that marked meeting places or pilgrimage routes. There is little evidence that they were associated with burials. Celtic crosses frequently had a circular piece surrounding the intersection of the vertical shaft and the shorter cross pieces, these are the 'wheelhead' crosses. They may be relatively plain but were usually carved all over with complex abstract patterns, interlocking forms of ribbons, knots and spirals, together with stylised flora and fauna motifs. The most developed form of cross contained figure sculpture of Christ and the saints. Owing to a lack of documentary evidence, it is rarely possible to date these crosses accurately.

The most outstanding of the English crosses sits among the wide open rolling hills of the Scottish border

Mawgan-in-Pydar, Cornwall. The late tenth-century 'wheelhead' cross is the most beautiful of the many decorated crosses in the county. It is 5 feet (1.5 metres) high with a diminutive figure of Christ in high relief. The other sides are decorated with corded knotwork.

country, in the churchyard of the isolated hamlet of Bewcastle, Cumbria. This is the area where Columba and his monks entered England. The crosshead is unfortunately missing but the shaft, standing about 14 feet (4.25 metres) high above a plinth, is decorated on all four sides with a unique variety of sculpture: sacred figures, animals, foliage and abstract work in the form of knotted interlace. The cross has been dated to around 700–750, the earliest period of this type of art in England. 'The quality of the work is extremely high. There is nothing more perfect of a comparable date in the whole of Europe. The figures are beautifully calm, classically dressed and posed' – all of which indicates a sculptor of Romano-Celtic culture.

At the other end of the country, Cornwall remained a stronghold of Celtic people who resisted Anglo-Saxon invasions until the ninth century. The cross at Mawgan-in-Pydar, four miles (6.4 kilometres) north-east of Newquay, is one of the most impressive in a county rich in such structures. It is of the wheelhead or four-holed type, carved from a single 5-foot-high piece of local Pentewan stone. The tapering shaft has a moving carving of a miniature Christ in high relief and there is characteristic interlace on the side with a small piece of runic lettering at the bottom. The date is perhaps tenth century.

INTERIOR SCULPTURE

When Anglo-Saxon churches were enlarged in later centuries, as most were, some of the Saxon sculpture was happily preserved and repositioned on the new walls.

Inglesham, Wiltshire, has a late Saxon Madonna and Child which captures the love of a mother for her infant. The finger of God, above, points down to His Son.

The large and ambitiously appointed church at Wirksworth, Derbyshire has a 6-foot (1.85-metre) Saxon coffin lid now mounted on an aisle wall. Created in about the year 800, '[i]t is one of the most interesting sculptural remains of its date' and is covered overall with New Testament scenes. A small section of two scenes is illustrated on page 15, showing the Ascension of Christ and the Annunciation of the Virgin Mary. This coffin must once have held the body of an extremely important person.

At Romsey, Hampshire, the Normans replaced a Saxon nunnery with a grand abbey which possesses two Crucifixions taken from the nunnery, one inside and one on an outside wall. The former is a 'very valuable piece' of the late tenth century or early eleventh century showing the Virgin Mary and St John below the cross-arms and two Roman soldiers beneath, one piercing the side of Christ with a lance as described in the Gospels (John 19:28–35).

The village of Breedon-on-the-Hill, Leicestershire, is actually at the bottom of the hill but its church is dramatically outlined against the skyline on the broad flat top. The Venerable Bede (673–735) in his *History of the English Peoples* described a minster church (a monastic church endowed by royal charter) here,

Inglesham, Wiltshire. A Saxon Virgin and Child of *c.*1000 captures the love of a mother for her child while the finger of God points down to His son.

[continued on page 16]

Breedon-on-the-Hill, Leicestershire. The church contains the largest collection 'of the most interesting Saxon sculpture in England, *c*.800'. The subjects and styles are so different as to be clearly by sculptors of different artistic cultures and times.
Clockwise from top left: Three saints; two figures holding branches; a female saint with a book, possibly the Virgin Mary; a frieze of weird pot-bellied and horned animals.

Sompting, West Sussex. An abbot with a crozier, late Saxon. The classical arch shows cultural connections with Rome.

Romsey Abbey, Hampshire. 'A very valuable' early eleventh-century Crucifixion scene. Two angels are on the arms of the cross with the Virgin Mary and St John on each side. Beneath them are two soldiers, one piercing the side of Christ with a lance, the other offering him a sponge with vinegar (John 19:28–35).

2

NORMAN ENGLAND: A NEW SCULPTURE OF POWER AND DOMINATION

The Norman People, Their Character, Architecture and Art

Iffley church, Oxfordshire, exudes the heavy power of even the smaller Norman village churches and even at a distance the abundant use of sculptural decoration is apparent.

Within twenty years of William of Normandy's victory at the Battle of Hastings on 14 October 1066, the Anglo-Saxon England described in the first chapter had changed forever. The majority of the people were still of course of Saxon descent, but forms of government, hierarchical structures and land ownership were totally Norman: by this time only two per cent of the old Saxon nobility were in possession of their lands, the rest now being held by Norman barons as tenants-in-chief of King William. Meanwhile, the landscape was transformed by a great wave of building: cathedrals of monumental size and grandeur and thousands of parish churches large and small – as well as numerous castles. How did all this come about?

At the time of their invasion of England the Normans had been in Normandy only since round the year 900, having arrived from Norway as part of the long series of raids by the Vikings on the countries bordering the North Sea. They were quickly accepted by treaty with the French king and settled peacefully. Originally pagans and with a culture very different from those of France and England, this people accepted and then wholeheartedly embraced Christianity – including a special loyalty to the popes in Rome. However, they did not lose their fundamental character: dynamic, strong-minded, inventive, militarist and expansionist. A potent urge to conquer and colonise new territory remained.

Above: These two arches show the large variety of abstract geometrical sculpture used by the Normans: the ubiquitous zigzag and bobbins, wheels, pellets and trellis work.
Left: Northampton, St Peter. The inside tower arch has in addition beaked bird-like heads and a dragon on the capitals.
Right: Hales, Norfolk, the outer north doorway.

Below: Northampton, St Peter. Two capitals in the north arcade again show the inventive imagination of the sculptors. There is an abundance of delicate vine trails and corded strands which surround two dog-like animals, left, and grotesque heads, right.

NORMAN ARCHITECTURE AND ART

In the tenth and eleventh centuries, architecture and art in southern Europe, particularly the south of France, had been transformed by development of the style known as Romanesque based on the designs and building techniques of Imperial Rome. All over France, cities and towns were transformed by the building of vast cathedrals, abbeys and parish churches which exuded strength and self-confidence in their massive solidity. Their decorative details had a similarly forceful, vibrant character. Buildings of this type must have appealed to the Norman psyche, and comparable buildings soon went up across the province of Normandy. It was this Romanesque, or their version of it, that the Normans brought to England and which so changed the landscape, where it is generally known as the Norman style of architecture.

It is tempting to think of the transformation wrought by the Normans as a more advanced civilisation with better and more efficient government and more sophisticated art forms replacing a primitive society of inferior culture. But on the contrary, under Alfred the Great (r. 871–901), who built on the work of his predecessors, there had been the beginnings of Anglo-Saxon England as a nation that was well

The arch capitals at Leominster Priory, Herefordshire, have interesting cameos of real life and mythology. **Clockwise from top right:** A Green Man with leaves issuing from his mouth was a symbol of fertility used throughout the Middle Ages; two men planting a tree; two lions fighting.

Tympanums, the areas within a doorway arch were widely used to illustrate biblical scenes. Stretton Sugwas, Herefordshire. Samson rides a horse.

Aston Eyre, Shropshire. The entry of Christ into Jerusalem on an ass.

Etton, East Yorkshire. Two sculptures in high relief. St Peter with keys.

St Paul with sword.

governed and well financed under a rule of Christian justice – even if during the next 150 years this was interrupted by Viking invasions and some incompetent kings. Its cultural artefacts in many forms, including the sculpture discussed in the preceding chapter, was of the highest quality, at times the best in Europe. Nonetheless, there is no mistaking the dramatic difference between Saxon and Norman architecture and art, as the accompanying illustrations show. Given the solidity of Romanesque buildings and the skill

of the Norman masons, a great deal of their work has survived in thousands of churches, sometimes as complete buildings and in many others which have been extended in later centuries but retain many of their original features and character.

NORMAN SCULPTURE AND FURNISHINGS

Sculpture as we use the word today in terms of freestanding statuary is rare in Norman art. Instead,

Four of the many hundreds of Norman fonts that generations of church people have retained over the centuries. They vary greatly in style and design.
Clockwise from top left:
Laneast, Cornwall. Wheels and human heads are carved in Cornish granite.
Bodmin, Cornwall. A complex architectural type structure with much floral decoration and heads.
Bledlow, Buckinghamshire. A refined, almost classical design. The cup-shaped bowl is fluted with almond shapes above and there is a decorated base.
Anstey, Hertfordshire. An extraordinary composition in which four mermen hold their split tails all around the bowl. Norman sculptors had a strange ability to mix the sacred, the secular and mythological fantasy in their work.

Two fonts of the famous Herefordshire school of Romanesque sculpture. **Above:** Eardisley. Left: two men fighting ferociously with a sword and an axe. The context is unknown. Right: the Harrowing of Hell, in which Christ, recently resurrected from the dead, pulls two people into heaven.

Below: Castle Frome. Left: the baptism of Christ by John the Baptist in the River Jordan. Right: two affronted doves.

sculpture was used as an integral part of the architecture, in order to decorate and enliven the heavy masses of masonry associated with Romanesque buildings. This work takes many forms: abstract geometrical, floral and, most interestingly, human figures and animals, often engaged in lively action scenes. The sculptors had a liking too for grotesque and mythological varieties of human and animal forms, deriving in part from their Scandinavian origins. The architectural features decorated in this way were doorways (prominently visible of course to all entering), chancel arches (which faced the congregations throughout services) and the arches and capitals of the arcades which separated nave from aisles.

The only sculpted freestanding furnishings are the fonts, which survive in remarkably large numbers. It is not unusual to see these in churches today, still wholly or partly in the original Norman state. More surprising is to see a Norman font in a building that otherwise belongs to later medieval periods. It is as though at each stage of rebuilding, the congregations were reluctant to throw away an item at which they, their parents and grandparents – and many generations before that – had been christened. These fonts employed the full repertoire of Norman imagination and decoration, a small sample of which is illustrated.

No account of Norman sculpture, however brief, should fail to mention the Herefordshire school of Romanesque sculpture. The Norman kings fortified the English border against the Welsh with a line of castles, large and small, many of which are now situated in remote Herefordshire countryside. These castles were provided with chapels, some of which now serve as village parish churches. The Marcher Lords who commanded the castles were men of battle, not of culture or intellect, but they employed high stewards to organise their non-military affairs, choosing men of education, well travelled throughout Europe and beyond, and in contact with bishops, abbots and other senior churchmen. Between the years 1120 and 1160, these men in turn employed two remarkable sculptors, their names unknown, to decorate their various churches. Not only is the work of great technical and artistic skill, it is informed by erudite knowledge of theological and biblical references, much of this taking symbolic form. The sculpture adorns all the church features mentioned above but it is perhaps the fonts that are the most remarkable – those at two village churches are illustrated.

Over the period between 1066 and 1200, the Normans left an enduring and instantly recognisable mark on English churches, from the largest cathedrals to the smallest parish churches.

3
STAINED GLASS AT CANTERBURY CATHEDRAL, 1180–1220

Transcendent Radiance Comes to English Churches

THE INSPIRATION OF A FRENCH ABBOT

Something just as novel and radical as the first wave of Norman influence came to England from northern France in the closing years of the Norman period. The effect of this was to endure with few breaks as an integral part of our churches right up to the present time. For 1,000 years, stained glass has played a significant role in churches as a means of teaching, but equally importantly in creating an inspiring atmosphere of transcendent radiance and holiness. For this we have to thank especially a twelfth-century abbot who ruled over the Abbey of Saint-Denis north of Paris, the equivalent of England's Westminster Abbey.

In the 1140s, Abbot Suger (1081–1151) decided to rebuild the eastern end of his ancient but decaying abbey church. He employed an unknown architect who effectively created the Gothic style. New structural techniques were used to replace the heavy massiveness of the Romanesque with lighter structures, which among other things enabled stone walls to be opened up with much greater areas of glass. But Abbot Suger was to make his own personal contribution too. Glass, clear and coloured, had been created and used since the times of ancient civilisations and small amounts of stained glass were employed in Norman and even Saxon churches. Suger knew that from the earliest days the Christian church regarded Christ as *Lumen Mundi*, The Light of the World (John 1:4–5), and Suger's own spirituality developed this idea of the affinity between God and light, particularly through the magnificence of coloured lights. He wrote in 'De Administratione':

The loveliness of many coloured gems and glasses has called me away from external cares, and worthy meditation has induced me to reflect, transferring what is material to that which is immaterial. Amidst this light and colour it seems to me that I am dwelling as it were in a strange region of the universe which exists neither in the slime of the earth nor entirely in the purity of heaven and that by the grace of God I can be transferred from this inferior to that higher world.

Even today, putting aside modern scientific knowledge of electromagnetic radiation, the common perception of light is of something ethereal, spiritual, beyond material things. Another essential element of Suger's thinking was that coloured glass could be made to create sacred pictures based on the Old and New Testaments and the lives of the saints, for the teaching of largely illiterate people.

Suger brought together a team of craftsman and artists of the highest calibre to create his glass. There were the men who made the clear glass and then coloured it by the addition of mineral compounds to get the right hues and brilliance, processes requiring great technical skill and judgement. Meanwhile, the artists drew the outline of the required picture using charcoal on a white-painted table. The glass was cut to fit and the pieces held together with grooved strips of lead. The dark outlines of the latter provide the strong delineations between, say, the parts of a body, head, arms and legs, that are characteristic of stained glass. In the twelfth century, the two groups of workers thus created a high art, one of richly glowing

[continued on page 29]

Opposite: The Trinity chapel at the east end of Canterbury Cathedral containing the Becket shrine and much of the twelfth- and thirteenth-century stained glass.

One of the Old Testament windows (see also pages 28–29): *Adam Delving* or digging the land after his expulsion from the Garden of Eden is perhaps the best-known stained-glass picture in England (Photo by Angelo Hornak/Corbis via Getty Images).

Above: St Thomas Becket was murdered in the cathedral in 1170 and his tomb was at the centre of the shrine and the encircling 'Miracle Windows'. His unflinching gaze tells of his resistance to the demands of Henry II.

Top right: Pilgrims on the road to Canterbury. A journey such as this was the subject of Geoffrey Chaucer's *Canterbury Tales*, written in the late fourteenth century.

Middle right: A priest, mourners and coffin at a funeral at the shrine.

Right: Two scenes of pilgrims praying at the cloth-covered shrine in 1220.

colours and beautifully designed and characterised pictures. Never bettered, it spread throughout France and soon to England.

STAINED GLASS AT CANTERBURY CATHEDRAL

St Augustine and his monks, who arrived in Kent in 597 (see Chapter 1), established the first cathedral at Canterbury and Augustine became the first archbishop, in effect if not in name. (In 2021 the Most Reverend Justin Welby is the 150th holder of that title.) The Saxon cathedral was rebuilt in 1070 by the first Norman archbishop, Lanfranc. Thomas Becket, the 40th archbishop, was murdered there in 1170 at the orders of Henry II, following a long feud between the two. The east end was destroyed by fire in 1174. The monks employed a Frenchman, William of Sens, for the rebuilding and it was he who brought the Gothic style to England – here in a work of novel and outstanding beauty.

The easternmost part of the rebuilding, beyond the choir and high altar, now known as the Trinity Chapel, was conceived as a tomb and shrine for Thomas Becket who had been canonised soon after his death in 1173. In the medieval tradition of great churches, it became a place of pilgrimage – the most popular in England in fact, where people from all over the country and from mainland Europe came to venerate the saint and seek miracle cures. The whole area was fitted with stained glass made in northern France and French glaziers came to design and make the windows in situ between around 1180 and 1220. The workmanship is hence of a quantity and quality that has not been surpassed in England. The glaziers used deep blues, reds and greens made by adding ores of cobalt, copper and chromium respectively to the clear molten glass to produce richly glowing effects. The whole space is an unforgettable jewelbox of colour, just as Abbot Suger had created in his chancel at Saint-Denis about thirty years previously. The subject matter falls into two broad categories: windows showing scenes from the Old and New Testament, and the Miracle Windows.

The People of the Bible

Two of the biblical windows are illustrated. The most famous and the most widely reproduced is the image of 'Adam delving' (i.e. digging), in which the first man

Another of the Old Testament windows: showing the ancestors of Christ. **From left to right:** Lamech, Noah, Thara, Jared and Methuselah. All have animated poses with alertly cocked heads and excellently done draperies.

Above: Audrey of Canterbury is cured of a quartan fever.

Left: Two cures each shown as a 'before and after' pair. Top, left and right: An unnamed woman is brought before a priest, is healed and rises up to give thanks. Bottom, left and right: Mad Henry of Fordwich is cured and gives thanks.

Opposite: Six circular panels show a number of cures. **Top pair.** Left: William of Kellet's leg is healed. Right: he goes away rejoicing. **Middle pair.** Left: Adam the forrester is shot by a poacher with an arrow in the centre of the picture. Right: a man on a stretcher drinks water from the shrine. **Bottom pair.** Left: a sick man in bed. Right: Adam the forrester, previously, is cured and leaves an offering of thanks at the shrine.

is made to work for his living after being expelled from the Garden of Eden following his disobedience to God. The second is a group of five later Old Testament figures shown seated under a line of arches, 'the poses animated, the heads turned or cocked alertly, the hands in expressive gestures. The draperies are excellently managed in a multitude of folds.'

The Miracle Windows

The original tomb and shrine of St Thomas that stood at the centre of the Trinity Chapel was destroyed by order of Henry VIII in 1539. A simple candle resting on the floor at this spot is constantly alight as a perpetual reminder. The Miracle Windows are still arranged in a large semi-circle in the surrounding walls; they are so called because they record life at the shrine at the time it was built. St Thomas himself is portrayed as a stern and uncompromising figure, as indeed he was. Some windows show pilgrims on horseback or on foot making their way to the cathedral, but the majority tell the stories of ordinary people who came to the shrine seeking cures for physical and mental illnesses through the intercession of St Thomas in heaven. Some are single scenes; others are in the form of a 'strip cartoon' of several images: a person at home sick, coming to and praying at the shrine, being cured and going away while giving thanks and a donation in return. The last element was very important. One cartoon was intended as a warning: a man is cured, makes no offering, returns home and is there struck down by yet another serious illness! The names and home places of the pilgrims are given beneath the pictures in small Gothic lettering.

It was intended that pilgrims should be able to follow the story as they travelled around the circumference of the space. Consequently, they are positioned at a height that can also be conveniently seen and enjoyed by modern visitors – and recorded by modern photographers.

Only a small selection of the scenes can be illustrated. Detailed study of these lively and charming cameos can take some time but one leaves with a real feeling of life in thirteenth-century Canterbury and an admiration for a high point in the art of stained glass making.

4
MEDIEVAL MUSICIANS AT BEVERLEY, EAST YORKSHIRE

MUSIC HAS PLAYED AN IMPORTANT role in Christian worship from the earliest times. In the pre-Reformation English Church, Gregorian chant was the norm for liturgical music in cathedral and abbey churches, and in Catholic countries has continued to be so. In the post-medieval period, composers of many nations wrote masses, anthems, oratorios and motets for church services. At the level of everyday worship, Victorian and later composers have created a vast repertoire of hymns. In the late twentieth and early twenty-first centuries, a wide range of music for Evangelical and gospel groups has been significant, as well as the young Christian pop culture.

It is not surprising that artists have wanted to portray the musicians who performed in churches. The most popular medium has been stained glass, and the most

The South view of the minster. Its great size, two pairs of transepts, twin west towers and interior treasures compare with any English cathedral.

Above left: A gittern was the ancestor of the modern guitar, and was first depicted in the thirteenth century. This instrument could be plucked with the fingers or a quill and was popular with court musicians, minstrels and amateurs.

Above right: A vielle, the medieval version of the modern violin, with 3–5 gut strings tuned with frontal pegs.

Left: Two pipes being blown simultaneously.

Opposite page:

Top left: Bagpipes are now regarded in Britain as characteristically Scottish but for centuries they have been played in mainland Europe, North Africa and western Asia.

Top right: Tabor pipes date from the eleventh century. They have only three holes, so that they can be played with one hand while the other is used to beat the tabor or drum.

Bottom left: A handbell would give a sound redolent of the great bells that rang out from medieval towers.

Bottom right: Two drums.

popular subjects have been angels playing harps, lutes, trumpets, tambourines and so forth. Victorian glass features much of this. Carvings in stone are far less common, particularly when they show human musicians, and even rarer when they depict complete bands.

The little market town of Beverley, East Yorkshire, has a minster church dating from the twelfth to the fifteenth century, although it is on the site of an eighth-century Saxon foundation. In size and grandeur this church rivals some of the finest cathedrals in the country and has many treasures of outstanding quality. The early fourteenth-century Percy tomb has been considered 'the most splendid of all British decorated funerary monuments'. The choir stalls of 1520 have intricately carved canopies and sixty-eight misericords involving scenes from everyday life.

In terms of human interest, however, the most memorable feature at Beverley is on the inside wall of the north aisle, below the windows, where it can be seen and enjoyed (and photographed) at leisure. A long line of fourteenth-century stone carvings shows local men playing a variety of stringed, wind and percussion instruments – the medieval forerunners of those used today. Each carving is a charming and lively cameo of music making. If this band played in the minster (and why otherwise would these carvings be present?), it must have produced a musical experience very different from the solemn, sonorous sounds usually heard in the building.

Yet another group of musicians, in this case singers, is also portrayed in Beverley (shown on page ii). A short distance from the minster, separated by streets lined with eighteenth-century houses and shops, is the parish church of St Mary, well known as one of the largest and most beautiful in all of England. In 1520 a new nave arcade in this church was paid for by various people of all ranks, in the medieval tradition. Some have their names inscribed on the capitals but one group, 'the mynstrells', opted to have themselves portrayed together in the form of a carving on the capital of the bay they had paid for. Unlike those at the minster, the capital is painted in glorious colour. These figures are a heart-warming and jolly group who will bring a smile to the face of any visitor to this stunning building. Even the staid academic Pevsner was moved, writing of 'a famous funny and lovable group'.

The vernacular music of the common people was obviously a popular feature in medieval Beverley.

Above: The 'portative' or portable organ was one of the most popular instruments between the thirteenth and sixteenth centuries. Supported by a sling, it could be carried in religious processions. The left hand pumped a sheepskin bellows, while the right hand played a button-type keyboard of two octaves. Because of the limited air supply, it could sound only one note at a time.

Opposite: The tracery form of decoration used by medieval woodcarvers reflected that used by stonemasons in their window heads. The forms differed significantly in the succeeding periods of Gothic architecture.
Left: Flowing window tracery of the Decorated Gothic period, c.1290–1330, is characterised by complex sinuous forms which were infinitely variable.
Right: Tracery of the Perpendicular Gothic period, c.1330–1550, is characterised by the repeated use of vertical mullions which give the style its name. It offers fewer opportunities for variation.
Both these examples are at Bunbury, Cheshire, carved from the local New Red Sandstone.

5
MASTERPIECES OF MEDIEVAL WOODCARVING

Six Norfolk Screens

O F ALL WOODEN CHURCH FURNISHINGS, the rood screens are the most exquisite examples of the medieval woodcarver's art, happily in places where they can be so easily seen and enjoyed.

Gothic architecture and art are characterised by the prolific use of decoration known as tracery, in both stonework and woodwork. From the thirteenth century onwards Gothic windows became increasingly large,

following a desire for ever more light. The lower section of a window, the larger part, consisted of vertically straight mullions (supporting or decorative divisions between units of a window or screen) to hold the glass. Rather than simply continue these into the pointed arch above, the masons found it aesthetically pleasing to fill the space within the arch with an open 'crochet-like' mesh of stonework which held smaller pieces of glass.

The screens of the later or flowing period of Decorated Gothic, *c.*1290–1330, are characterised by tracery which is sinuously complex and varied. It provided the woodcarvers with unlimited scope for imaginative designs in the same way as did window tracery for the stonecarvers of the period.
Right: Holme Hale. The entrance section of the rood screen into the chancel has two rose windows of exquisite design.
Below left: Merton. The rood screen is 'excellent with very fine and dainty, thornily cusped tracery'.
Below right: Taverham. A screen of exceptional delicacy made into an altar rail after the Reformation.

The screens of the Perpendicular Gothic period, c.1330–1550, are characterised by an emphasis on vertical mullions, many of which rise to meet the containing arch. The result is slightly more uniform screens than the Decorated work but still allowing for variation. These screens also echo the work of the stonemasons in Perpendicular window tracery.
Left: Hemsptead. A 'good' screen with two-light divisions with prominent ogee arches.
Below left: Beeston. A north aisle screen of 'superb quality' with thickly crocketed ogee arches and close tracery.
Below right: Worstead. This includes exquisite coving which joins the screen to the top beam, equally ornamented.

This tracery reflected the style of architecture at the time. The use of tracery began in the second, 'Decorated' period of Gothic, around 1250–1330, and continued uninterrupted into the 'Perpendicular' period of Gothic (c.1330 to 1550). The Decorated falls into two very easily distinguishable sub-periods, Geometrical tracery of about 1250 to 1290 and Flowing tracery of around 1290 to 1330. In the former period, tracery is based on the circle and its quadrants, a quite simple and easily analysable form. In Flowing tracery, this gives way to much more complex, sinuous shapes, which allow the mason free imaginative and creative rein. Perpendicular tracery is created by allowing some of the principal mullions from the lower, main part of the window to continue to the top of the pointed arch, together with shorter perpendiculars created within the arch itself. This gives a strong sense of verticality, which accords the tracery its name.

The woodcarvers copied the techniques of stone tracery when constructing rood screens. These screens usually separated chancels from naves in medieval churches. The bottom part of the screen was a solid dado, generally painted with images of saints (see Chapter 6), rising to about 4 feet (1.2 metres). Above this was an open traceried section completed by a forward-projecting cornice. The rood itself stood within a rood loft, which surmounted the structure. It consisted of a large crucifix with images of the Virgin Mary and St John the Evangelist on opposite sides. This was the most prominent set of images visible to the congregation during services, but they were ruthlessly destroyed during the Tudor Reformation. The screens below, however, have survived in large numbers – particularly in the southern counties of Norfolk, Suffolk, Devon, Somerset and Cornwall.

It is well known that Norfolk medieval churches are more numerous and more richly endowed with furnishings, especially wood furnishings, than any other county and this includes the rood screens. H. Munro Cautley in his incomparable descriptions and gazetteer *Norfolk Churches*, now long out of print, lists and describes two hundred and two medieval Norfolk screens. Of this large number, six have been chosen for inclusion here, three with Decorated tracery and three with Perpendicular.

6

THE CONTRIBUTION OF
THE MEDIEVAL PAINTERS

THE WORK OF STONEMASONS, GLAZIERS and woodcarvers has been described in the three previous chapters. All artists wished to showcase their work in churches and medieval painters left few surfaces of stone or wood without colour, although this is very little in evidence today. Two periods of the Reformation saw a massive amount of destruction of this decoration: the reign of Edward VI in the sixteenth century and that of the Cromwellian Commonwealth in the seventeenth century. Most of the paintings were figure studies of people in the Old and New Testaments and the later saints; this evidence of popish superstition and idolatry was abhorred by zealous Protestants and puritans. From the evidence we do have today, paintings of outstanding artistic merit were rare in parish churches – there is only one in this collection – but it has already been emphasised that the work of simple craftsmen can still provide as much

The oldest Christian work of art in England, which pre-dates the Middle Ages, is at Lullingstone Villa, Kent, the home of a wealthy Christian Roman. It was painted c.400 and depicts two people in the *orans* (i.e. praying) position in what was possibly a private chapel in the villa (Carole Raddato/CC BY SA 2.0).

enjoyment and instruction as that of the leading artists. The very rarity of medieval paintings contributes to their importance, as does the insight they give into the minds and religious attitudes of ordinary people in towns and villages.

Medieval church paintings should not be thought of simply as a form of adornment. For the painters and the clergy who employed them, this work, like that of the glaziers, was less for decoration than for instruction and cultivating religious devotion at a time when most people were illiterate and without books. The works described here are confined to figure studies on walls and wooden screens. It is rare to find paintings on roofs in parish churches where the detail and teaching effect

Left: Claverley, Staffordshire. A section of a long 50 × 5 feet (approx. 15 × 1.5 metres) mural above the north arcade. Painted c.1200, it shows groups of armed knights on horseback facing each other. 'It is one of the most important of its date in England' and may represent the Battle of the Virtues and the Vices.

Below: Little Kimble, Buckinghamshire. A small church with one of the best collections of wall paintings in England.
Left: St George and the dragon and rescued princess behind him.
Right: The entombment of a female saint by an angel.

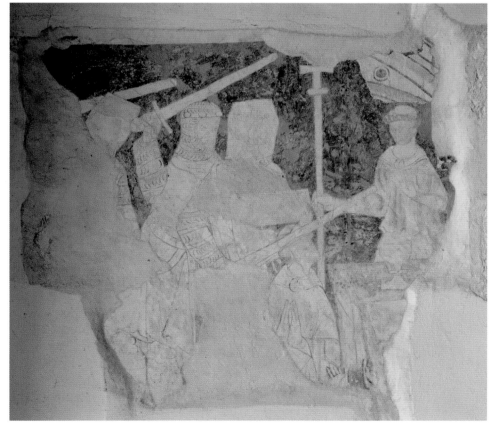

would be largely lost, although colouring of some kind could be applied there too.

WALL PAINTINGS

The remains of these are particularly rare and fragmentary as during the Reformation it was easy to obliterate them under a coat of whitewash. Modern maintenance work occasionally reveals traces, and in the hands of expert conservationists these have been painstakingly revealed and conserved. Iconoclasm was not the only cause of their disappearance; wall paintings are the most fragile of all church artworks, as they were applied on plaster-coated stone walls and buildings without heating or damp courses and so would naturally disintegrate with time. As such they would never have been expected to last more than a generation, after which they would have been renewed in the same way that we redecorate a house today. The painters would apply their materials to plaster that had first been moistened. The pigments were simple: various oxides of iron gave red and yellow ochre; copper ores gave green or blue; charcoal gave black or shades of grey when mixed with lime. Skilful blending of these could provide a greater range of colours. The pigments were stirred into lime-saturated water and applied with a brush. A degree of fixing could be achieved with skimmed milk which contains casein. Because of the wide areas of wall available to the painters, they often specialised in large 'action' scenes involving several people.

SCREEN PAINTINGS

The upper, traceried parts of the rood screens separating chancels from naves have been described in Chapter 5. The panel dados, the lowest solid parts, were invariably painted with sacred figures: Christ, the Virgin Mary, the apostles and doctors of the church. The later saints were very popular too, especially those who were patrons of particular groups of people or those associated with the curing of certain diseases. The oil-based pigments used by the painters here were more extensive than those of the wall painters, with a wide range of bright colours including extensive use of gold (yellow) in halos and clothing.

Two wall paintings, both c.1400.
Above: Edingthorpe, Norfolk. A 'good' St Christopher carrying the infant Christ.
Left: Brookland, Kent. The murder of St Thomas Becket, centre kneeling, with three assassin knights, left, and a priest, right.

The finest and most precious work of art illustrated is an altar reredos or retable of around 1330 in the small and remote village church of Thornham Parva, Suffolk. It was discovered in nearby Thornham hall and brought here in 1927. It measures around 12 × 3 feet (about 3.5 by 1 metres) and is mounted behind the altar table in the same position for which it would have been originally made, as the focal point of the church. It consists of four saintly figures on each side of a Crucifixion on a gilded oak panel. The gently swaying figures point to a date within the later Decorated period of Gothic. The two end figures on each side (not shown) include

Dominican monks and this suggests that the work was made for a Dominican friary in East Anglia, possibly Thetford. In a beautifully illustrated guide to the retable, Paul Binski remarks: 'It is one of the most miraculous survivals of art of the English Middle Ages … the second oldest to survive and one of only a handful in the country. Two others are to be found in Westminster Abbey and Norwich Cathedral.' The largesse of the donor and the trustful generosity of the parish people in displaying it, with appropriate security, mean that it now stands not in an art gallery or museum but in a place where it fulfils its original purpose as an aid to Christian worship.

Two rood screens each with two apostles.
Right: Edingthorpe, Norfolk. On the left we have St Bartholomew with a skinner's flaying knife, with which he was said to have been martyred. On the right is St Andrew with saltire.

Previous page: Southwold, Suffolk.
Left: St Philip, believed to have been crucified.
Right: St Matthew with tax collector's money bag.

Ashton, Devon.
Above: Parclose screen with Old Testament prophets in sixteenth-century dress and with animated expressions.
Left: Rood screen with, left to right, St John the Baptist holding an Agnus Dei; Virgin and Child; St George and Dragon; St Mary Magdalene with box of ointment.

Thornham Parva, Suffolk. A very rare and beautiful altar retable of c.1330 originally in a local abbey church. Lost at the Reformation, found and donated here for its original purpose in 1927. This central section shows, left to right, St John the Baptist with Agnus Dei; St Peter with keys; Crucifixion with Virgin Mary and St John; St Paul with sword; St Edmund, martyred Saxon king killed with an arrow.

Strensham, Worcestershire. A former rood screen converted into the west gallery front which spans the entire width of the nave. Four of the twenty-three saints showing, left to right, St Erasmus patron of sailors with spit or cutlass; St Lawrence with gridiron; St Stephen with stones used to kill him; St Anthony of Egypt with a pig, his symbol.

7
VILLAGE LIFE (I): A YEAR IN THE LIFE OF MEDIEVAL PEASANTS

Carvings on the Choir Seats of a Village Church

T HE VILLAGE OF RIPPLE IS in an enviable position in the south-west corner of Worcestershire, where it meets Herefordshire and Gloucestershire. Its compact cluster of houses away from main roads enjoys peace without isolation. The large parish church is surrounded on two sides by village cottages, by a capacious eighteenth-century former rectory and its grounds on the third and by

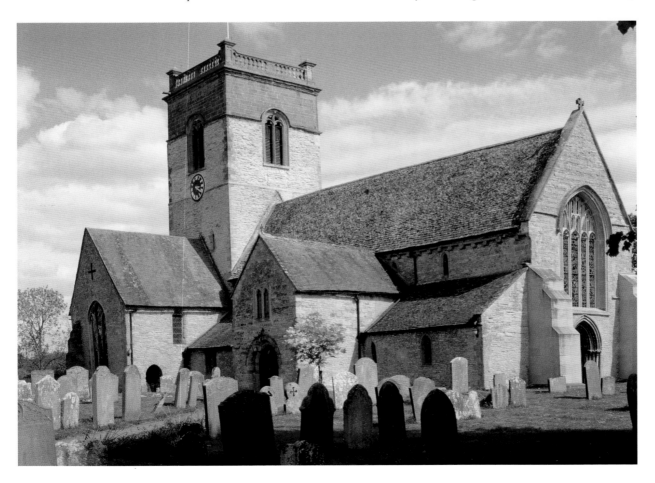

North-west view of the church. Originally Norman, it was enlarged several times in the later Middle Ages.

January. Collecting large tree branches for firewood.

February. Splitting wood to make fences.

March. Sowing seeds from a basket. A horse pulls a harrow that covers the seeds with soil.

April. Scaring birds away from growing seeds with noise-making devices.

May. Not a labour of the month but the image of the Virgin Mary, to whom the month was dedicated. She is shown blessing the fields and crops.

June. A man on a horse goes hawking (the bird has broken off).

July. Two men with staves guard a bakery with the oven door above and a loaf of bread below (perhaps there was a shortage of flour at the time).

August. A man with a sickle and a woman with a crook reaping.

September. Collecting corn for malting.

October. Beating down acorns for pigs.

November. Killing a pig to be salted for winter.

December. Alongside a fire with a cooking pot, a man helps a woman with her spinning.

open fields on the fourth — a fine combination of all aspects of rural life. The building has a cruciform plan with a central crossing tower. Various parts date from 1180–1530, an evolving story typical of thousands of village churches. The chancel has furnishings of outstanding human interest. Before the Reformation, the church was staffed by a non-monastic community of Augustinian canons. For the recitation of the daily offices they required a set of choir stalls which are placed on three sides of the chancel, sixteen in all. These have happily survived the turmoil of English church history. Their misericords, the undersides of the tip-up seats, have a remarkably rare and complete set of fifteenth-century carvings of the 'Labours of the Months' — a familiar theme in medieval art which describes the monthly tasks carried out by peasants in England, outdoors and indoors, from January to December. The twelve cameo carvings are by an unknown local craftsman, competently carved 'in a delightfully lively manner' with intriguing details of the everyday life of the poorest class of medieval society. The fact that the kneelers and fronts of the stalls have been removed means that visitors can enjoy these cameos closeup at leisure and in comfort, whereas in many places misericord carvings can be examined only in cramped surroundings.

We see in churches a great deal of material recording the lives of the great and the rich and much of this is enjoyable, but to be in touching distance of the work of a fifteenth-century woodcarver telling the stories of his fellow villagers is an especially moving experience in the silent peace of a fine church.

8
VILLAGE LIFE (II): MEDIEVAL LIFE FROM BIRTH TO DEATH

Carvings on a Norfolk Village Font

IN CHAPTER 5, NORFOLK ROOD screens were used to illustrate the splendour of medieval woodcarving. The county's fonts are equally as numerous and impressive. They are generally remembered by visitors for their tall pulley-operated covers and canopies, which are as finely and intricately carved as the screens. Another type known as 'Seven Sacrament' fonts is of considerable artistic and historical interest and almost confined to East Anglia. The medieval Roman Catholic church recognised seven sacraments as instituted by Christ, just as it does today: baptism, confirmation, the Eucharist (Mass), penance or confession (now known as the sacrament of reconciliation), marriage, ordination and extreme unction or the last rites, now known as the sacrament of the sick. (At the Reformation the Church of England in its Thirty-Nine Articles and the Book of Common Prayer recognised only two of these: baptism and the Eucharist.) Late medieval sculptors and the clergy who employed them realised that the eight sides of an octagonal font (the usual shape) could be used to accommodate carvings of the seven sacraments, with the eighth side used for a Crucifixion or Baptism of Christ. Just forty of these fonts survive in England – twenty-five in Norfolk and thirteen in neighbouring Suffolk. A large number were destroyed or defaced at the Reformation for theological reasons as well as the dislike of religious imagery. Of those that survive the best preserved is at Sloley, well off the beaten tourist trails about twelve miles (19 kilometres) north-east of Norwich, where the village church is of typical flint and limestone. The groups of little figures are charming cameos of some of the most moving moments in human life, from birth to marriage to death. The obvious youth of the recipients depicted is striking, the confirmands, the grooms and brides and even the ordinands; this was a time when forty years was a good life expectancy, people were married in their mid-teens and a third of all children died before the age of five.

For the historically minded at a christening service today, it must be singularly rewarding to be gathered around a piece of stonework that depicts the same service being conducted in the same way over 500 years ago. And general visitors here, as at Ripple (see Chapter 7), are brought face to face with images of people not so very different from themselves which were carved by a man who would have seen at first hand the events of everyday life that he was depicting. This is the evidence of history at its most compelling.

South-east view of the limestone and flint church, fourteenth and fifteenth century.

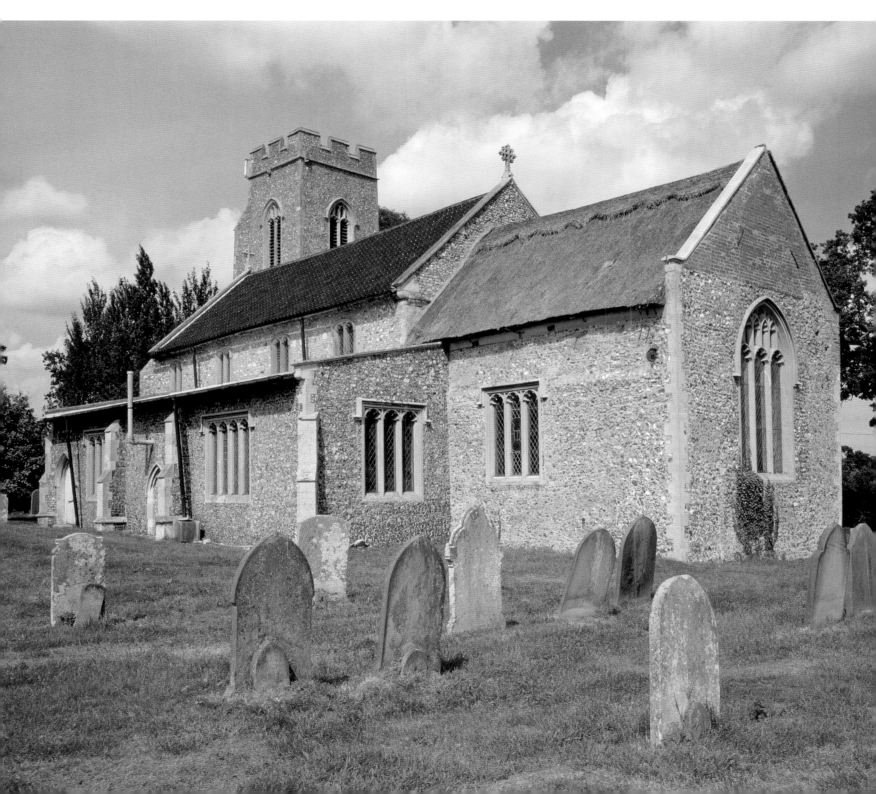

Baptism. A priest appears to immerse an infant fully while an assistant holds a service book and the family looks on.

Confirmation. A bishop and priest with very young recipients.

Eucharist. A priest celebrates mass with boy altar-servers and a bell-ringer to sound for the sanctus and consecration.

Penance or Confession. In the left foreground, a seated priest and kneeling penitent. On the right, an angel kicks away the devil shown as a dragon. The three figures behind are not eavesdroppers but perhaps represent the three conditions for the sacrament: contrition, confession and absolution.

Marriage. A priest with a very young groom and bride – a commonplace in the Middle Ages.

Ordination. Candidates kneel before a bishop with assistant clergy.

Extreme Unction or anointing of the sick. A priest with the family at the bedside of the dying person.

The eighth side shows the Baptism of Christ by John the Baptist in the River Jordan.

The archetypal medieval and immediate post-medieval monuments were those of the deceased recumbent on a tomb chest. This one is in English alabaster, a stone particularly suited

It is a unique and memorable experience to enter a church like this, lonely and quiet, with yourself as the only visitor. Furthermore, it is not necessary to be psychic or a spiritualist to feel the almost tangible presence of those men and women, recumbent on their tomb chests or towering above you on wall

with the grandees of the past and to remember that everyone, no matter how wealthy or famous, will eventually come to dust like them.

Architectural historians generally give accounts of English monumental sculpture in art-historical

AN INTRODUCTION TO THE MONUMENTS

(Chapters 9–12)

ONUMENTS TO THE DEAD ARE the most prominent features in many English churches (but not of course the most important in terms of their pastoral function). The range is immense in terms of age, size and quality. At one end of the spectrum are small wall tablets with an inscription and a little decoration, sometimes very well done. At the other end are monuments that rise from floor to ceiling with one or more life-size figures and architectural surrounds in the form of canopies or reredoses with classical columns and pediments. They may be of native limestones or sandstones, or imported white or coloured marbles. In the medieval and post-medieval periods the sandstones and limestones were often brightly painted and gilded, bringing colour to an otherwise sombre interior.

The earliest monuments originating in the late eleventh century after the Norman Conquest consist of stone coffin lids laid into the floor and inscribed with foliated crosses and other simple decoration. In the twelfth century, the first effigies were cut into the surface in very low relief and not projecting above it. The deceased so memorialised were generally bishops or abbots in cathedrals or abbey churches. The first fully three-dimensional effigies appear in the thirteenth century and now included royalty, nobility and their attendant knights. They lie on tomb chests implying but not actually containing a body. Most have their hands piously joined in prayer, except for the knights who may grasp their swords. In looking at the people commemorated in this way over the next four chapters, we are of course seeing the great and the good – and not so good – of English society. Below

royalty and nobility their status descends no lower than the squirearchy, the gentry and professional classes. However, an intentional balance has been kept in this volume, where in previous chapters the lives of working-class people have been portrayed in stone, wood and glass.

Sometimes a church may contain only a single or just a few monuments of consequence. The high points of church explorations are reached in parish churches that serve villages adjacent to some stately home and park where a family or a succession of families have lived for several centuries. While these families of dukes, marquesses or earls may have kept London houses, they regarded their real homes as here in these rural places where they lived and ruled and where they wished to be buried and remembered close to the 'big house'. So over the centuries a parish church, often quite a modest building in itself, becomes as much a family mausoleum as a local place of worship. The monuments can fill every part of the building. The most prestigious location was the chancel but from here they spread into transepts, aisles and naves. When these were full, special side-chapels could be built to accommodate the overflow. The monuments in such places represent every period in turn, with their associated styles of architecture and sculpture. The artistic quality of the latter does not correspond with the humble character of the church but with the wealth of those buried here. The aristocratic families could afford to commission the finest sculptors of their time, such as those whose work appears in the two great 'mausoleum churches' of England:

9
THE MONUMENTS (I)

The Theatre of Piety

HE THEATRE OF PIETY is the name given here to the monuments of the Middle Ages, the Age of Faith, and the immediate post-medieval period. This faith was very much a real and committed one, even when it lived alongside intolerance and appalling violence and cruelty. From 1250 to 1550 most monuments took a standard form where the deceased lie recumbent on tomb chests. There is little attempt at real portraiture and the outline of the body is

completely hidden under clothing. The most significant features of these effigies are the hands piously joined in prayer. This sends out two messages to the viewer: that the deceased was a devout Christian and one who would enjoin the prayers of others to hasten the journey of his or her soul from purgatory to heaven. The people remembered in this way are bishops, priests and abbots who lie alone, and aristocratic laity who lie alongside their spouses.

Boxgrove Priory, Sussex. Lord De La Warre, d.1526, and his wife. The most prominent of all 'piety' monuments were the chantry chapels, small stone cages, buildings within a building, where masses were said daily for the soul of the deceased. It is unusual for lay people to be so treated. The beautifully ornate structure is a marriage of Gothic and Renaissance forms just when the latter were entering England.

We know very few of the names of the sculptors in the earlier part of this period, despite the supreme skill of many of them. They worked in English stones, the limestones (including the near-black Purbeck marble from the Dorset coast) and sandstone which may be left plain or brightly painted and gilded. Alabaster mined in Nottinghamshire and Derbyshire was very appropriate for funerary work as the ashen grey colours of some varieties have the waxy appearance of the dead.

A feature often included on the tomb chests is a group of 'weepers', that is, mourners in the form of children of the deceased. They may be cut in low relief on the sides of the chest or may be shown in full three-dimensional form prominent at the head or feet of their parents, sometimes vying with them for prominence (they would, after all, be the ones paying the sculptor).

The hands of the weepers, like those of their parents, are also piously joined in prayer.

The recumbent tomb chest type continued into the reigns of Elizabeth I and James I, but a new type emerged in addition. The effigies now rise up a stage to emulate kneeling positions at a prie-dieu, a type of prayer desk, either singly or as a couple facing each other. Both types are now almost invariably in bright colours.

These monuments of piety cover a period of about four hundred years, so that the dresses and headgear of the lay people are a good record of changing fashions and styles for historians.

In the late seventeenth and eighteenth century, this aura of piety would change completely into a worldly secularism until revived again in the nineteenth century (see Chapter 16).

Above: Moreton Corbet, Shropshire. Sir Richard Corbet, d.1567, and his wife with animals at their feet. A good example of how plain limestone or sandstone can be given a brilliant painted effect.

Left: Warwick, St Mary. Richard Beauchamp, Earl of Warwick, d.1439. A very rare brass effigy surrounded by a brass cage on a Purbeck marble chest in the church's famous Beauchamp Chapel, one of the most famous mausoleums in England.

Opposite: Mereworth Kent. Sir Francis Fane, d.1590, and his wife lie within a classical architectural surround. Above, two angels hover to welcome them into heaven. This is a good example of how the simple effigy-on-a-chest monument could be turned into something grander.

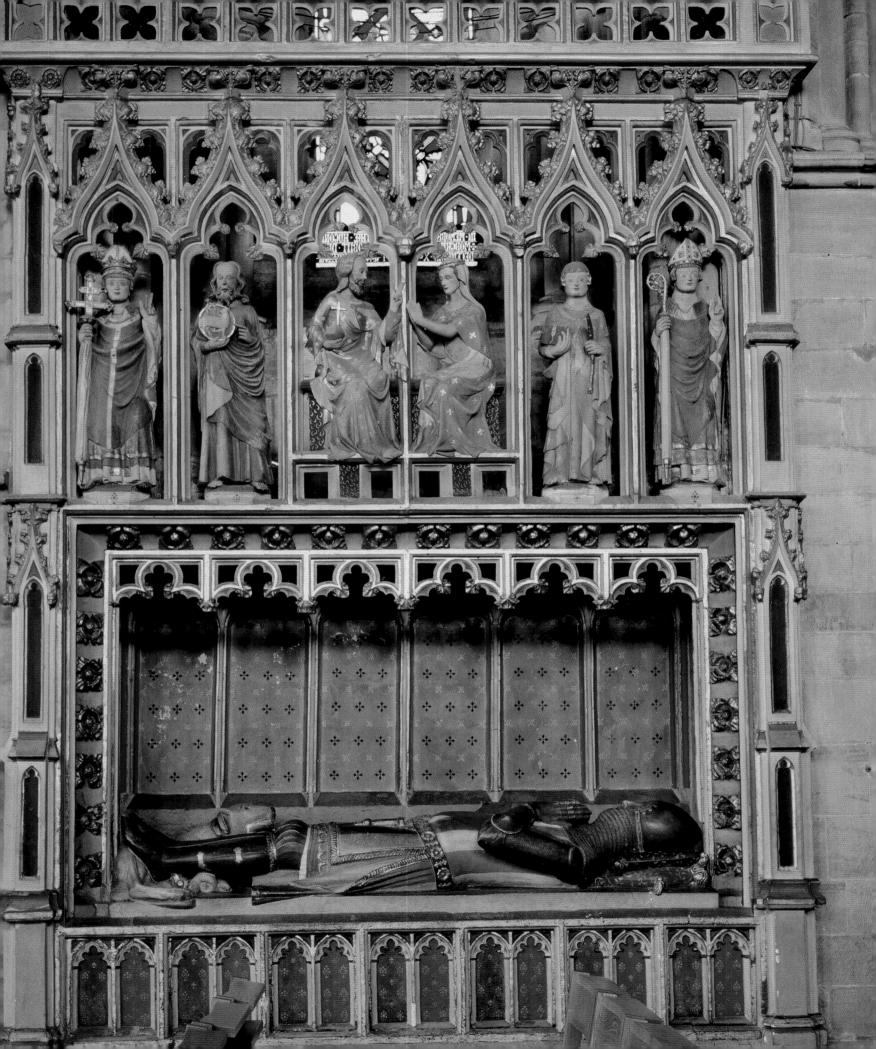

Previous page: Hereford Cathedral. Another example of how a simple tomb chest monument could be made grander. Here, Sir Peter de Grandisson, d.1352, lies in armour below canopied figures where at the centre Christ crowns his mother Mary as Queen of Heaven.

Three good examples of tomb chests with 'weepers', i.e. family members, usually sons and daughters of the deceased, who are shown kneeling and praying for the souls of their parents.

Clockwise from above:

Framlingham, Suffolk. The sons of Henry Howard, Earl of Surrey, executed 1547 by Henry VIII for treason.

Exton, Leicestershire. Sir Robert Kelway, d.1580 and his daughter. His son corresponds at his feet. Exquisitely carved throughout in alabaster.

Morley, Derbyshire, Katherine Babington, d.1543, is mourned by her eight praying sons. 'Competently and sensitively carved, the monument might well be in Westminster Abbey.'

Left: Ludlow, St Lawrence, Shropshire. Edward Waties, d.1635, and his wife face each other kneeling at a prie-dieu. This colourful pious type was ubiquitous throughout the later sixteenth and early seventeenth centuries. A strange mask-head looks down on them.

Below: Framlingham, Suffolk. Sir Robert Hitchin, d.1631. Only residual traces of Christian piety are retained here, where four angels guard the black marble tomb slab supported in the centre by an urn.

10

THE MONUMENTS (II)

The Theatre of Pomp and Pride

MANY OF THE ENGLISH ARISTOCRACY within the hierarchy of dukes, marquesses, earls, viscounts and barons served their country well as politicians, statesmen and administrators. Others lived out their days in comfortable obscurity. As owners of vast estates (amounting to hundreds of thousands of acres in some cases) they ruled the lives and fortunes of tens of thousands of tenants, sometimes with fairness, sometimes with heartless indifference. However, what most of them had in common, whether distinguished or obscure, was a pride in their ancestry and the length of their titled lineages. Although common to almost any period, this characteristic reached an apogee in the eighteenth and nineteenth centuries. This is marvellously reflected in the family monuments erected at this time, as structures of awesome size and quality were created by leading sculptors of the day when English sculpture was at its most distinguished and money was no object. As previously remarked, when looking at the accompanying photographs readers might imagine themselves to be standing in Westminster Abbey, St Paul's Cathedral or one of the major medieval religious buildings. In fact readers must envisage themselves in some quite modest parish church close to the stately ancestral home of the deceased, deep in the heart of the English countryside. The house may well be open to the public now, so that house and church make up an enjoyable and informative tour as the places of life and death of a prominent family.

The monuments from the late seventeenth to the early nineteenth century stand in clear contrast to those of earlier medieval monuments (Chapter 9), which often surround them in a church which has been virtually a family mausoleum for hundreds of years. Gone now is any sense of piety, symbolised by hands joined in prayer. Rather, the effigies — either singly or more usually in family groups — stand erect with swaggering lordly gestures or lounge seated at ease. Native sandstones and limestones were now out of fashion. Based on the newly rediscovered appeal of classical antiquity, the sculptors worked exclusively in gleaming white imported marbles of the type their clients would have seen in the statues of the pagan Roman world during their Grand Tours of Italy. This appeal extended to the widespread conceit of showing the deceased in Roman dress. The monuments frequently have a reredos (but not now a complete canopy) of classical architecture with columns and pediments.

Sculptors from the Low Countries and France dominate monuments of the eighteenth century in England. Two stand out: John Michael Rysbrack (1694–1770) was born in Antwerp and trained in Rome before coming to England. His work is a combination of the calm antique classical and the theatrical Baroque; but the greatest sculptor ever to work in England was Louis-François Roubiliac (1702–1762), a Frenchman who trained in Lyon and Germany before coming to England. He worked in the new Rococo style, something a little lighter in mood than the Baroque or classical. Roubiliac was a superb portraitist of faces, catching real mood rather than stylised nobility. His figures were equally realistic, often informal, with large compositions and

[continued on page 71]

65

Elmley Castle, Worcestershire. The 1st Earl of Coventry, d.1699. The bewigged reclining figure wishes all to know of his status as he points to his earl's coronet.

Right: Coxwold, North Yorkshire. The Earl of Fauconberg, d.1700, with his father, left, in Roman dress. The latter appears to wave farewell to the world while five cherub angels hover above, two of whom prepare to replace an earthly coronet with a heavenly version. Modesty was never an aristocratic characteristic.

Opposite: Exton, Leicestershire. Baptist Hicks, 3rd Viscount Camden, d.1683. He stands with his fourth wife while three previous wives and their nineteen children surround them in medallions. By Grinling Gibbons, a rare example of a major sculpture by the great woodcarver. The theatricality of the poses and the curtains drawn aside are typically Baroque.

Opposite: Gayhurst, Buckinghamshire. Sir Nathan Wright, d.1721, and his son, right. 'One of the grandest and most successful of its type in England'. Sir Nathan was Lord Keeper of the Great Seal of England which he holds in his left hand.

Right: Stapleford, Leicestershire. 1st Earl of Harborough, d.1722. J. M. Rysbrack's 'superb' monument rises from floor to ceiling. The earl is reclining in Roman costume. At his feet are Lady Harborough and her infant child, 'a beautifully carved group'.

full of dramatic movement. He turned the chancel of Warkton church, Northamptonshire, into a grand theatre for the monuments of the Dukes of Montagu. Others included Peter Scheemakers (1691–1781), also from Antwerp, distinguished but not of the same technical skill or imagination as Roubiliac. Grinling Gibbons, although born in Holland of a Dutch mother, was a leader among the English sculptors, but his work in stone never achieved the sublime quality of his creations in wood (see Chapter 13).

The inscriptions on eighteenth-century monuments are worth reading – if one has the time. Interminable eulogies ascribe to the deceased every possible virtue, every degree of education, learning and wisdom, and every 'amiable' quality of character.

These 'Pomp and Pride' monuments are a breathtaking insight into the lives and attitudes of those at the top of eighteenth-century English society and the art of those who served them in death.

Previous page: Great Witley, Worcestershire. The 1st Lord Foley, d.1733. By J. M. Rysbrack, it is 'one of the largest funerary monuments in England'. The base platform alone is 6 feet high (1.8 metres). He sits reclining on a sarcophagus, his wife and an infant child at a higher level. Four of their seven children are included.

Left: Ossington, Nottinghamshire. William Denison, d.1782. A wealthy wool merchant and although he is the only non-aristocrat in this collection, he was able to afford an 'accomplished' statue by Joseph Nollekens, one wholly worldly in attitude and features.

Above and opposite: Warkton, Northamptonshire. The church is close to Boughton House, the great stately home of the Dukes of Montagu since 1683. These two monuments are two of four that fill the whole of the chancel, which was specially rebuilt to hold them. Each sits on a tall platform within a giant recess, two facing two. This is perhaps the most awesome and unified piece of theatre of great monuments in England.
Above: John, 2nd Duke of Montagu, d.1752. An incomparable masterpiece by L. F. Roubiliac. Near the centre is a medallion of the duke which is being fixed in place by a putto-boy helped by a life-size figure of Charity holding two children. At ground level his duchess is bent in grief.

Mary, Duchess of the 2nd Duke, opposite, d.1753. Also by Roubiliac. At the centre, two putti place garlands on an urn. Slightly below these are the three Fates of Greek mythology who govern the destinies of all mortals, two seated and one standing. Poignantly, a little naked boy crouches on the ground.

11
THE MONUMENTS (III)

The Theatre of War

I T MAY SEEM STRANGE THAT Christian churches, the centres of worship for a religion ostensibly existing to preach peace and love, should contain so many monuments to fighting men. Unfortunately, Christians have been as much inclined as any other group to wage war among themselves or with people of other faiths. (The fifteenth century, the last century of the Christian Middle Ages has been described as 'the bloodiest, cruellest and most corrupt in English history'.) Yet in defence of the presence in churches of military monuments, it can be argued that they glorify not war itself but the self-sacrificing courage of people often fighting for the freedom of others.

The military monuments here cover a very wide period, from the thirteenth to the late nineteenth century, and portray so many different kinds of people in sculpture so varied that any introductory generalisations are impossible. These photographs and their captions, presented in historical order, speak for themselves.

The memorials of those who fell in the wars of the twentieth century are described in Chapter 18, for reasons given there.

Above: Dorchester on Thames, Oxfordshire. A knight of *c.*1280. An unusually animated pose in which he is vigorously drawing his sword, with his shield in the foreground. A dog, symbol of fidelity, lies below his cross-legged feet. It is 'one of the finest and best preserved pieces of thirteenth century funerary in England'.

Right: Ashbourne, Derbyshire. Sir John Cockayne, d.1447, is dressed in chainmail armour in a monument carved in Derbyshire alabaster. Angels support his pillow. In a long and chequered career he fought under Henry V in the Hundred Years War and was High Sheriff of Derbyshire.

Three soldiers of the time of the English Civil War.
Clockwise from top right:
St Mary's, Ross-on-Wye, Herefordshire. Colonel William Rudhall, d.1651. A royalist soldier dressed in Roman military uniform.
Standish, St Wilfrid, Lancashire. Captain Edward Chisnall, d.1653, was a soldier in the royalist army. The delightfully colourful Baroque style tablet shows swords, a lance and a trumpet.
Broad Hinton, Wiltshire. Colonel Francis Glanville, a royalist soldier killed at the Battle of Bridgewater, 1645.

Above: St Anthony in Roseland, Cornwall. Two monuments to a seafaring family in this waterside church.
Left: Admiral Sir Richard Spry, d.1775. The wall monument shows Britannia in high relief sitting in front of a ship in low relief.
Right: Admiral Thomas Spry, d.1828 was a nephew of Richard and fought at the Battle of Trafalgar in 1805. A sailor and a woman stand beside a pedestal holding a collection of weapons and flags.

Left: Beverley Minster, East Yorkshire. Major-General B. F. Bowes killed in the Peninsular War, 1812. An angel inscribes *pro patria* in a book surrounded by cannon and cannon balls. Earlier he had fought in America, Gibraltar and Portugal.

Above left: Gaddesby, Leicestershire. Colonel E. H. Cheney, d.1848. A life-size piece 'more suited to St Paul's Cathedral than a village church'. He fought at the Battle of Waterloo in 1815, where four horses were shot beneath him.

Above right: Stanford-on-Avon, Northamptonshire. Edmund Verney Edgell of the 17th Lancers Regiment who was killed in 1879 at Ulundi, the last battle of the Anglo-Zulu War. He is shown laying a wreath for his fallen comrades.

Right: Lichfield Cathedral. Monument to the 80th Foot Regiment of the Staffordshire Volunteers who were killed in the Anglo-Sikh War in the Punjab, 1845–46. They carry the coffin of a dead comrade.

12
THE MONUMENTS (IV)

The Theatre of Pathos

IN THE EIGHTEENTH CENTURY SOME of the great family group monuments (see Chapter 10) showed grieving figures, but these played a secondary role to the proud poses of the central figures of the deceased. The grieving duchess of the 2nd Duke of Montagu at Warkton, Northamptonshire, is a piteous figure but she stands outside and below the main tableau (see page 72). The widow of Viscount Newhaven at Drayton Beauchamp, Buckinghamshire (see page 81) does the same. Monuments that show grief and mourning as the principal theme appeared in the late eighteenth century but their heyday was in

LEI·CHE'I·CIEL·NE·MOSTRA·TERRA·N'ASCONDE·

LE·CRESPE·CHIOME·D'OR·PVRO·LVCENTE·
E'L·LAMPEGGIAR·DELL·ANGELICO·RISO·
CHE·SOLEAN·FAR·IN·TERRA·VN·PARADISO·
POCA·POLVERE·SON·CHE·NVLLA·SENTE·

These pages: The deathbeds of two infants at times when such mortality was high. Left: Ashbourne, Derbyshire. Penelope Boothby, d.1791 aged 5 years, was the daughter of Sir Brooke and Dame Sussanah Boothby. The monument is one of the most famous in England. In life the child was painted by Sir Joshua Reynolds and Sir John Millais and sculpted in death by Thomas Banks. An inscription is written in the four languages she is said (by her parents) to have spoken. The monument was exhibited at the Royal Academy in London where Queen Charlotte, wife of George III is said to have wept.

the first half of the nineteenth century, the Regency to the early Victorian periods. The subjects include infants alone on deathbeds and pre-adolescent children dying in the presence of their parents. The most numerous, however, are husbands and wives grieving their spouses in deathbed scenes with attendant children. A more classical take shows a mourner before a broken column (a symbol of life cut short) or a funerary urn. The use of pure white marble continued from the eighteenth century as the principal stone. Francis Leggatt Chantrey (1781–1841) and Richard Westmacott (1775–1856) were two of the leading sculptors who specialised in this type of monument. The former produced them in hundreds — so many in fact that he

St Michael's, Ledbury, Herefordshire. John Hamilton, d.1851 aged one year, is guarded by two angels. The monument was exhibited at the Great Exhibition at Crystal Palace in 1851.

delegated much of the cutting of the marble to students in his studio. These pieces were smaller and easier to execute than the great Pomp and Pride monuments of the eighteenth century, so their affordability now extended downwards to the minor gentry and professional classes. Alongside some outstanding work, there is much from this period that has the feeling of mass production in the way of repetitive designs and mechanical execution, but nonetheless, these monuments have the power to evoke feelings of compassion in the modern viewer.

Top, left and right: The deaths of two older children. Left: Great Mitton, Lancashire. Richard Shireburn, d.1702 aged 9 years, contemplates a skull on the ground as angels hover above. The family lived at nearby Stonyhurst Hall. Right: Lichfield Cathedral. The two sisters Ellen-Jane and Marianne Robinson, who died of scarlet fever in 1812, were the daughters of one of the cathedral's prebendaries. Sculpted by Francis Chantrey, it attracted national interest like the Boothby monument twenty years before (see page 78).

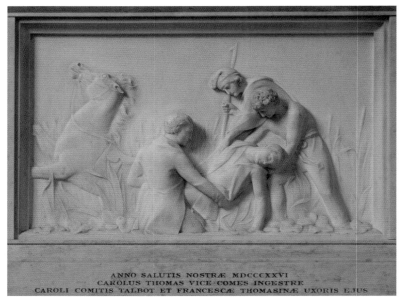

ANNO SALUTIS NOSTRÆ MDCCCXXVI
CAROLUS THOMAS VICE-COMES INGESTRE
CAROLI COMITIS TALBOT ET FRANCESCÆ THOMASINÆ UXORIS EJUS

TO THE MEMORY OF
PERCY BYSSHE SHELLEY,
POET,
BORN AT FIELD PLACE IN THE COUNTY OF SUSSEX, AUGUST 4. 1792.
DROWNED BY THE UPSETTING OF HIS BOAT IN THE GULF OF SPEZZIA JULY. 1822.
HIS ASHES ARE INTERRED IN THE PROTESTANT BURIAL GROUND AT ROME.
ALSO TO THE MEMORY OF

Bottom: Two monuments recording deaths in accidents. **Left:** Ingestre, Staffordshire. Viscount Ingestre died in 1826 aged 23 years when he was thrown by his horse. In this low-relief tablet by Francis Chantrey he is shown being helped by a friend and two workmen while the rearing horse is on the left.

Right: Christchurch Priory, Hampshire. Percy Bysshe Shelley drowned in 1822 aged 30 years in a storm in the Adriatic. The poet's wife is shown holding his recovered body on a beach where it was cremated in the presence of Lord Byron and others.

Drayton Beauchamp, Buckinghamshire. The Earl of Newhaven on his deathbed in 1728, with his grieving Countess. Such pathos is rare in early eighteenth-century monuments which are dominated more by pomp and pride (see Chapter 10).

Belton, Lincolnshire. The 1st Lord Brownlow, 1807. Sculpted by Richard Westmacott, a woman grieves by a broken column draped with foliage. The type was widely used 1760–1820, when the broken pillar represented human mortality.

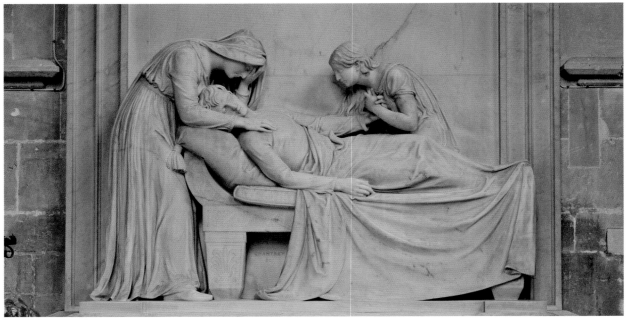

Edington, Wiltshire. Sir Simon Taylor, d.1815. The mother and sister of the bachelor grieve as he lies dying. Yet another by Chantrey.

Great Tew, Oxfordshire. Mary Anne Boulton, d.1829 aged 34 years. Another by Francis Chantrey, this conveys more feeling than most of its kind as the young woman gazing pensively beyond the open book contemplates her death. The exposed page reads: 'Thy Will Be Done.'

know · that · my   Redeemer · liveth

Angels at the scene of the deaths of adults as well as children were a common feature of Victorian monuments.
Left: Stanford-on-Avon, Northamptonshire. Lady Braye, d.1862. A woman with a cross and a book prays beside the deceased with angels above.
Opposite: Holme Lacy, Herefordshire. The naval Captain Scudamore Stanhope, d.1871. Death is represented by an anchor on a seabed as an angel directs his spirit to heaven.

IN MEMORY OF
CHANDOS SCUDAMORE STANHOPE, CAPTAIN, R.N.,
SECOND SON OF SIR EDWYN FRANCIS SCUDAMORE STANHOPE, OF HOLME LACY, BART.
BORN JANUARY 19TH 1823, DIED JULY 7TH 1871
AT MALTA WHEN IN COMMAND OF H.M. IRONCLAD SHIP CALEDONIA

13
JACOBEAN AND BAROQUE WOODWORK, 1600–1700

Post-medieval work, that created between 1600 and 1700, includes two periods that are readily distinguishable by very different types of craftsmanship and spirit: Stuart or 'Jacobean' work up to 1670, and Baroque from around 1670 to 1700 with some overlap. Because of the relative paucity of church building in the centuries following the Reformation, together with a lack of interest in existing buildings and their furnishings and the destructive 'restorations' of the Victorians (see Chapter 15), the quantity of woodwork in this period is not large.

Abbey Dore, Herefordshire, The Abbey church of St Mary. Chancel screen inserted c.1630. One of the largest and heaviest pieces of Jacobean furniture in England, with classical columns, spiky obelisks and heraldry.

Two examples of the aptly named 'horse-box' pews which had some popularity with aristocratic families in the mid-seventeenth century. They were designed to accommodate an entire family in privacy – a useful asset in times of social distancing.
Above: Kedleston, Suffolk. These double pews may have been for the family and an attendant household.
Right: Middleton, St Leonard, Greater Manchester.

Jacobean furniture is more likely to be seen in the manor houses of the time, these large and heavy oak pieces now dark with age: dining room tables and chairs, huge sideboards with their numerous little drawers and cupboards, often all surrounded by oak-panelled walls. Upstairs are the four-poster beds and other furniture. Decoration was much influenced by the Netherlands, with which there were extensive trading links. Gothic ornament had largely given way to the classical or at least a Netherlandish-English version thereof. Flat surfaces were decorated with much strapwork, interlaced bands or straps resembling fretwork. Three-dimensional decoration incorporated classical pilasters, capitals, urns and obelisks. Jacobean church furniture includes communion rails, altar tables, font covers, 'horse-box' pews, galleries and more, frequently inserted into earlier medieval churches.

Baroque architecture and art became fully developed in seventeenth-century Rome and flourished in southern European countries for some 150 years. It evolved when architects tired of the harmonious rule-based regularity of the early Renaissance and struck out into something more dramatic, or melodramatic, characterised by complexity and voluptuous sinuosity. Christopher Wren introduced the style into England, most notably in his City of London churches rebuilt after the Great Fire of 1666, but his was a calmer English version exploiting the opportunity for three-dimensional geometrical complexity (among other things he was a mathematician) without the voluptuousness of the Roman original. Wren employed the leading woodcarvers of the day to furnish the churches, men who readily adopted the Baroque to their craft. Outstanding among these were Grinling Gibbons, his colleagues and students. Their skills and the rich ornateness of their work was affordable to only a few and so Baroque furnishings are rare outside London.

Rycote, Oxfordshire. The entire church is filled with sumptuous furnishings dominated by two great family 'horse-box' pews, *c.*1630, next to the chancel, foreground. The one on the left has a domed canopy, the one on the right has a musicians' gallery above with its own staircase.

The mid-seventeenth century fitted many medieval stone fonts with elaborate wooden covers and canopies.
Left: Mendlesham, Suffolk. A beautiful canopy with multiple elements. **Right:** Astbury, Cheshire. A calmer, more classical structure with a combined canopy and cover. The latter is raised and lowered by a pulley.

Many pulpits were made in the seventeenth century, although not yet as prominent as the three-deckers of the eighteenth century (see Chapter 15). Most have panelled fronts with delicately carved abstract patterns repeated overall.

Left: Clun, Shropshire. This is the most typical of its kind, suitably simple but dignified for a village church. Right: Daresbury, Cheshire. This unusually elaborate piece has figure brackets and panels with balusters, cherubim, scrolls and guilloche.

City of London, St Mary Abchurch. The reredos of 1686 is by the master Baroque woodcarver himself, Grinling Gibbons. Corinthian columns carry a segmental pediment topped by four vases. The gilded limewood pelican is a symbol of the Eucharist. The centre section is surrounded by exquisitely carved garlands, a Gibbons trademark.

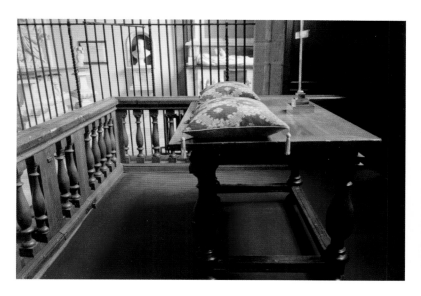

'Laudian' chancel furnishings at Ashburnham, Sussex. A sturdy altar table is surrounded on three sides by altar rails with dumb-bell balusters. The name derives from the furnishing (and wider) reforms instituted by Archbishop William Laud of Canterbury (1573–1645), who wished to restore the dignity and reverence due to the sacraments, which he felt had been demeaned by the growing Puritan wing of the Church of England in the mid-seventeenth century. He was executed in 1645 for opposing the will of a Puritan parliament.

City of London, St Mary Abchurch. This middle section of the pulpit of 1685 (there is a tall tester above) has the usual cherubs' heads and garlands. The stairs leading to it have a platform with twisted balusters. The whole structure is mounted on a 'wineglass' stem just visible.

City of London, St Mary Abchurch. One of the several handsome doorcases, which here leads to the tower. It is crowned by a gilded copper pelican.

City of London, St Stephen Walbrook. The stone font of 1679 has a wooden cover, its panels carved with tiny figures and foliage separated by twisted columns. There are little figures of the Virtues around the domed top which is surmounted by a gilded crown.

Beverley Minster, East Yorkshire. The inner face of the great west door, *c.*1700, has the figures of the four evangelists, Matthew, Mark, Luke and John, with their symbols below. It is a relatively rare example of large-scale Baroque work outside of London, possibly by Nicholas Hawksmoor.

City of London, St Stephen Walbrook. The altar rails have the ubiquitous twisted balusters but the top rail has unusual enrichment.

14
PORTRAIT OF A COTSWOLD CHURCHYARD

A Treasure Ground of Classical Elegance

Painswick Churchyard
The present church dates
from the late fourteenth
century, but the tall needle
spire was not added until
1632.

BEING IN THE CENTRE OF Gloucestershire, Painswick is approached from whatever direction through towns and villages built almost entirely of the Cotswold honey-coloured Jurassic limestone. So, it often surprises visitors to see that the stone throughout this village, in church, houses and cottages, is pure white – quite blindingly so on a sunny day – as if it were Portland limestone from the Dorset coast. But this local limestone was taken from quarries outside the village where, like Portland stone, it was laid down without incorporating those oxides of iron that give limestones elsewhere their buff colours. The prosperity of the Cotswolds that derived from the wool trade extended beyond the Middle Ages into the seventeenth and eighteenth centuries, and in those later times the residents were able to build an astonishingly large number of substantial houses characterised by the simple classical elegance that the eighteenth century did so well. This sense of prosperity and refined good taste gives Painswick more the character of a town than a village.

The church and its large churchyard are at the centre. The present building, with its tower and prominent, tall narrow spire, dates from about 1380 with various later additions. In the eighteenth century, houses were built around all four sides of the churchyard in a pleasing variety of sizes and detailing, thus creating a square with a fine open space at its heart. Pathways that cross the churchyard from its corners and sides take walkers from one street to another, so there is a happy sense

A glimpse of some of the large, elegant eighteenth-century houses that surround the churchyard on all sides.

Some of the ninety-nine smoothly clipped yew trees which divide up the churchyard into secluded areas.

Two of the chest-type tombstones with ornamental cherubs and festoons.

that the church is in the middle of the community, physically as well as spiritually.

In the late seventeenth century, the mason John Bryan established a successful practice here and his two sons John (1716–1787) and Joseph (1718–1780) continued the business. The two brothers were skilled stonecarvers as well as house builders and the wealthy merchants and professional people of the parish employed them in making family tombstones in the churchyard, which in number, elegance and variety surpass anything to be found in England. The local white stone they used matches that of the church and the houses around in perfect harmony, always the result when building materials follow local geology. The tombstones take several forms: chests and pedestals which can be square or hexagonal with straight, concave or convex sides, as well as columns and pyramids. The ornamental motifs reflect those favoured at the time: garlands, shells, torches, festoons and cherubs' heads. Memento mori in the form of skulls and whole skeletons take their place among these too. The stone is not of the most durable and there is inevitably a degree of erosion in the carvings, but they are still in a reasonable condition in this clean air. The Bryans erected handsome gateways into the churchyard, and there is a gatehouse and lychgate constructed in 1901 from old belfry timbers.

In 1792, ninety-nine yew trees were planted around the sides of the churchyard and to line the several pathways through it. These have grown into magnificent specimens, not allowed to spread as in many old churchyards but clipped annually in a smart orderly way to echo the elegance of the tombstones.

Throughout England there are innumerable beautiful churchyards, places of peace and serenity, places where nature and the human-made combine gracefully, places where the present keeps in touch with its past, but there is nothing else in England such as can be seen in Painswick.

15
EIGHTEENTH-CENTURY INTERIORS
Auditoriums for Preaching and Class Distinctions

ENGLISH CHURCHES' INTERIOR FURNISHINGS AND their arrangement in the eighteenth century were markedly different from the centuries immediately before and after. Before the Henrician Reformation which began in the early 1530s, the principal service in every church was the Mass or Eucharist, celebrated daily at a high altar and often also at side altars (a practice that continues today in Roman Catholic churches around the world). The altar was where the priest consecrated the bread and wine, which then became the Real Presence of Christ's body and blood. This most sacred event required the utmost reverence at a stone altar in a large and suitably furnished chancel. The latter was usually separated from the nave by a rood screen to emphasise its sanctity (see Chapters 5 and 6). The entire church was filled with statues, painted images (Chapter 6) and shrines to saints.

All this changed in stages during the reigns of Henry VIII's children, Edward VI and Elizabeth I. The doctrine of the Eucharist involving transubstantiation altered

Four three-decker pulpits (shown on pages 98–101) whose size and elegance emphasise the importance attached to preaching in the eighteenth-century Anglican Church.

Opposite: Salle, Norfolk. An example of how a tall Georgian three-decker pulpit could be inserted into a medieval church, in this case one considered by some to be the finest in England. Although the clergy have since preached from an eighteenth-century structure, the congregation has continued to be seated in the medieval benches with their poppy-head ends in the foreground – a typical example of how the centuries mix in English churches.

Left: Slaidburn, Lancashire. The 'uncommonly attractive' pulpit here also has its original soft furnishings.

and its celebration became less frequent. Chancels often became semi-redundant, with a simple wooden 'holy table' in place of a stone altar. Side-altars were abolished and any representation of Christ or the saints was deemed popish superstition, as were shrines and relics. A great deal of stained glass containing sacred iconography was also destroyed in this period.

Conversely, the role of Bible reading and preaching became greatly extended and church furnishings changed to reflect this. Large pulpits of a new three-decker type were installed and prominently placed. The lower deck was for the parish clerk, who led the responses to the prayers. The minister or 'parson' read the prayers and the appointed lesson from the second deck. He then climbed to the top deck to preach sermons of interminable length by modern standards, so bitingly satirised by the cartoons of William Hogarth. Each deck was usually fitted with its own lectern and small door. In existing medieval churches these were installed as the older furnishings were removed. In new churches built in the seventeenth and eighteenth centuries, these furnishings were installed from the start and as a result their interiors are more of a unified whole.

To accommodate congregations during the long sermons, it was necessary to have appropriate provision for seating. In the eighteenth century, the favoured arrangements were 'box pews' in which benches were enclosed on all four sides to a height of 4 to 6 feet (about 1.2–1.8 metres), with a door from the aisle to afford access for up to six people. Class distinctions quickly established themselves. For a noble family living in a nearby 'big house', an entire transept was reserved or a west gallery at the back of the church. These areas were well furnished, with upholstered chairs with tall backs of the type found in their houses, and in some cases even fireplaces were provided. In Shobdon church in Herefordshire, situated within the park of a stately home, the family occupied one transept furnished in this way, while their servants facing them in the opposite transept had plain benches – where attendance and behaviour could easily be monitored by their employers. In the main body of the church, the box pews were carefully graded in two or three stages: the tallest at the front for

[continued on page 106]

Left: Gibside, County Durham. Pulpit and altar are in 'the most perfect example of a Georgian church in the most select classical style'. As is usual for the time, the altar is dominated by the massive pulpit.

Opposite: Shobdon, Herefordshire. The whole interior including the pulpit is a unique 1752 'Rococo-Gothick' creation of Richard Bateman, a friend of Horace Walpole. The lower deck for the parish clerk is no more than a little chair. The velvet hangings are original.

Above: The priority of pulpits over altars is well demonstrated in these two extreme examples, where they completely block the view of the latter from many places in the church.
Left: King's Norton, Leicestershire. A parson's-eye view taken from the chancel. Church and furnishings are all of a piece of 1775.
Right: Chichester, St John, Sussex. The view on entering the church is of an unusual central pulpit in an apparently altar-less interior. The three decks are here separate pieces: the tall top deck on a 'wine-glass' stem is flanked by the lower and middle sections. The hidden altar behind is no more than a domestic table.

Left: A typically small Georgian altar and railed-off chancel at Pilling, Lancashire built in 1717.

If Georgian pulpits were large, so were the congregations by modern standards. Many churches built at the time were designed with elegant galleries to accommodate them and many existing medieval churches also had galleries introduced.

Above: Shrewsbury, St Chad. The fine circular church of 1790 has a gallery running round the whole interior.

Right: Edenfield, Lancashire. Although in an isolated Pennine village the church is large and the furnishings well made.

Well, Lincolnshire. The spectacularly sited parkland church was built in 1733 as an eye-catcher from the Hall. The Oxbridge-educated lordly builders of such places often requested an interior with the collegiate-type seating which they would have known from their undergraduate days, combined with a pulpit on a centre side-wall. The splendid mahogany furnishings enhance the equally exquisite plasterwork.

Tong, West Yorkshire. The class distinctions in eighteenth-century society are illustrated by the squire's box pew with its own fireplace at the front of the church. The box pews behind are lower and smaller.

Opposite: A print of 1736 by the satirist William Hogarth is titled 'The Sleeping Congregation'. It shows a short-sighted parson preaching from the top deck of his pulpit in the City of London, oblivious of his slumbering listeners below and above him. The parish clerk in the bottom deck, however, is wide awake, lasciviously eyeing the bosom of a sleeping woman (The Metropolitan Museum of Art, New York/Public Domain).

the squire, gentry and professional classes, and lower ones farther back for the wealthy tradespeople in the towns or farmers in the country. The doors of the box pews could have brass plates indicating their 'owners'. In wealthy town parishes or villages with rich church patrons, all these furnishings were of highly polished imported hardwoods. In poorer parishes, they would be made of plain or painted pinewoods. At the very back were plain backless benches for the lower classes.

At this time church attendance was high among all classes in town and country, with over half of the population going to church on Sundays. Ground-floor accommodation was insufficient to seat all and so galleries were inserted into medieval churches or built into the plans of new churches. They were allocated to the working classes and so had plain benches, usually tiered as in a theatre.

Before the advent of brightly coloured Victorian tiles, floors were made of large stone flags of limestone, sandstone or slate.

There is no doubt that all this provided a dignified, sober interior well suited to an equally dignified liturgy – albeit one better tailored to the educated class than many of the people.

From the middle of the nineteenth century, these interiors started to disappear slowly – for two reasons, one theological the other social. Firstly, the Oxford Movement, starting in the 1830s, sought to return the Church of England to its 'Catholic' roots, away from the predominantly 'Protestant' ethos of the time. The importance of the Eucharist was stressed within a more elaborate liturgy of ritual, hymns and vestments. Where this occurred, chancels regained their pre-Reformation status in which the Eucharist was celebrated weekly. Preaching times were reduced and three-decker pulpits were replaced by those in the contemporary type, the style with which we are most familiar today.

The second reason for change was the late Victorian realisation that the class distinctions inherent in the old seating arrangements were morally wrong when

Robin Hood's Bay, North Yorkshire. The perfectly preserved interior of 1821 in a moorland church is in complete contrast to Gibside, Well and others here with its plain pine woodwork throughout. However, all the essential features of the era are the same: box pews (one larger than the others), central pulpit and two-sided gallery. A tiny altar table is behind the camera's viewpoint.

practised in churches. So, box pews were swept away and replaced by the form of pews we have today. Eventually, degrees of 'churchmanship' would emerge, with the High (or Anglo-Catholic) church furnishings identical or close to the Roman Catholics, and the Low (or Evangelical) churches closer to the older dispensation, while the larger number of Broad churches fell somewhere between.

Despite everything, in a few remote village churches these changes were not wrought, either for reasons of religious conservatism or because of lack of funds. These 'unrestored' interiors, as they are known today, are an unexpected joy to modern church explorers. Here they enter a world where Jane Austen, her clerical characters and her readers would be entirely at home at matins or evensong. They see not only well-designed and crafted workmanship but a vivid in situ glimpse of English social history which constitutes another important treasure of the nation's churches.

Whitby, St Mary, North Yorkshire. This is the Georgian interior to outdo all others in England. Originally a Norman church close to the Abbey, transepts were added in the eighteenth century. Every available space is fitted with seating: box pews at ground level and tiered benches at gallery level. Even the transept, left, has a gallery. The pulpit in the foreground is the focal point of a preaching auditorium par excellence. The photograph is taken from a squire's box pew inserted as a bridge across the chancel arch, a demonstration of class that can only be regarded as unparalleled irreverent arrogance today. The normally austerely academic Pevsner wrote: 'When one enters it is hard to believe and impossible not to love. It is one of the churches one is fondest of in the whole of England. To whom do we own the infinite gratitude for never having gutted it?' Services take place in the holiday season only. (There are several other parish churches in the town.) For fear of fire, the densely packed gallery benches cannot, of course, be used today.

16
VICTORIAN INTERIORS: 'THE BEAUTY OF HOLINESS'

Creations of Polychromatic Brilliance

Cheadle, St Giles Roman Catholic, Staffordshire.
A. W. N. Pugin's masterpiece of 1846 was the seminal
work of the authentic Gothic Revival, the inspiration for
hundreds that followed. With the unlimited resources of
the Earl of Shrewsbury, every embellishment could be
lavished on the interior.
Previous page: Not only the furnishings but also the nave
piers are coloured overall.
Left: An Easter Sepulchre in the chancel for use in the
ceremonies between Maundy Thursday and Holy Saturday.

T HE LOVE OF COLOUR WAS a striking feature of
Victorian taste in the fittings and furnishings
of their buildings. The latter included new
parish churches (of which about six thousand were
built during the reign), the mansions of the rich and
the semi-detached houses that filled the expanding
suburbs. Even some of the small terraced houses of this
period have little pieces of stained glass in front doors
and windows. Brightly patterned tiles are everywhere,
around fireplaces and in hallways and bathrooms.
So it seems appropriate to choose colour as a basis
for bringing together the descriptions of the various
features of Victorian church interiors. Polychromatic
effects could extend to the exterior stonework and
brickwork (but in accordance with the principle of this
volume, architecture as such is not described at length).

The large number of churches built, along with
many others enlarged or extended, in Queen Victoria's
reign (1837–1901) can be taken as a measure of the
genuine religious revival and reform within both the
Evangelical (Low) and Anglo-Catholic (High) wings

of the Anglican Church. The eighteenth century was once described by John Betjeman as 'the century the Church of England went to sleep'. Now the clergy put new zeal into more frequent services that engaged with congregations of every background and education, while also carrying out a great deal of social work in fields such as education and the relief of poverty.

From the 1840s onwards, the movement for revival and reform was accompanied by huge changes in the interiors of Anglican churches. Three influences were behind this. One was theological, the second was sociological and the third was based on architectural taste (but with strong theological overtones).

As mentioned in Chapter 15, the first theological agent of change was the Oxford Movement starting in the 1830s, which created the Anglo-Catholic wing of the Church. Under the influence of the Oxford Movement, not only was the Eucharist now celebrated at least once a week but the setting for its celebration became more elaborate, with decorated altars and chancels, appropriate music in the form of anthems and hymns sung by vested choirs in the chancels accompanied by new organs. Candles, processional crosses and vestments were used and statuary appeared for the first time since the sixteenth century. Churches in the eighteenth century had mainly clear glass, with only a little stained glass left over in medieval churches

where it had escaped the iconoclasts. Stained glass with images from the Bible and of saints now reappeared in quantity. At first these things were confined only to the very High Church and indeed much opposed by the Broad and Low Church clergy, who abhorred the openly popish nature of the new furnishings and services. Gradually, however, the new theology spread to most parts of the church.

The second influence for change came from a new view of Christian society which was shared by all sections of the Church. It abhorred the blatant class distinction that had hitherto existed inside the buildings in the form of 'class-graded' seating in the reserved galleries, box pews and plain benches. These were abolished and replaced by the uniform arrangements we have today.

The third influence for change came from a radical switch in architectural taste, linked at least initially to theology. The seventeenth and eighteenth centuries had turned away from Gothic architecture, now thought of as culturally barbaric, in favour of the 'civilised' classical style of antiquity. Although medieval Gothic churches remained in abundance, new churches were now constructed to resemble the classical pagan temples of ancient Greece and Rome with the porticos, columns and pediments of the style. A passionate and articulate Roman Catholic convert, Augustus Welby Northmore

In churches built by wealthy benefactors, imported multicoloured marbles could be used structurally in certain prominent areas of the church.
Left: Skelton, North Yorkshire. Chancel shafting, 1876.
Right: Hoarwithy, Herefordshire. A pier supporting the dome, c.1885.

Pugin (1812–1852), fiercely opposed this pagan architecture for Christian use. For him, the Middle Ages were the ages of Faith and of the Gothic style. From this, he reasoned (with little logic) that the only style for Christian churches was Gothic. This thinking was accepted by a wide part of society, ecclesiastical and secular. Pugin's ideas naturally extended to the interiors of churches, where he advocated a similar return to medieval furnishings. This coincided with the theology of High Churchmen particularly, who even embraced the idea of rood screens and side-altars. Others accepted Gothic as a style rather than a theology.

Almost all of the new churches built after 1850 reflected these views. A large number of them were mediocre, dictated by the amount of money available. In wealthier parishes or those which had a wealthy benefactor such as a duke, earl, businessman or widow building in memory of a husband or son, it was possible to employ an architect of the highest calibre.

These included A. W. N. Pugin, George Gilbert Scott with the family dynasty succeeding him, and William Butterfield, George Frederick Bodley, William Burges and John Loughborough Pearson. As devout Christians, many of these men built with conviction as well as commercial professionalism at a time when a major church commission was a prestigious project.

The architect would commonly design all the furnishings and fittings, down to the last detail. Colour in the Gothic taste is a common connecting theme. In design and colour, to echo the idea of the 'Beauty of Holiness' (Psalm 96:9) was the aim of the architects and their patrons.

COLOURS IN STONE

A church might be built of limestone, sandstone or brick but decorative multicoloured (and expensive) polished marble imported from around the world could be used for pillars, friezes, altars, fonts and

Hoarwithy, Herefordshire. The white marble altar is inlaid with semi-precious stones, including lapis lazuli and tiger's-eye.

pulpits. In rare cases it extended to mosaics in the ancient Byzantine tradition for adorning domes or small areas of wall. Here the English versions are in the Arts and Crafts style.

COLOURS IN WINDOWS

The amount of Victorian glass inserted into the new churches or existing medieval ones during 'restorations' could fill several Amazon warehouses. A great deal is poor quality, mass-produced work. Dark, muddy colours make some churches caverns of gloom. Designs were, perhaps inevitably, repetitive with over-fussiness of detail as the designers attempted to use the same techniques as employed for painting on canvas. Even much of the work of C. E. Kempe (1834–1907),

the most popular and prolific glazier of the time, is of this type. Others, such as William Wailes (1808–1881), could go to the opposite extreme, dealing in acid-bright reds and yellows. The most outstanding work of the period, universally acknowledged as such, was made by William Morris (1834–1896), who founded the Arts and Crafts Movement, and Edward Burne-Jones (1833–1898), a member of the pre-Raphaelite Brotherhood. These men rejected mass-produced factory-made glass (and furniture, fabrics and much else), advocating instead a return to the medieval tradition of the same skilled craftsman designing and making all his own pieces of art. In their partnership of making stained glass, Burne-Jones would design the picture in monochrome and Morris would choose the colours, before cutting and composing the glass. In these windows they returned to the deep, glowing colours of the thirteenth century (see Chapter 3) and to simple designs in which the important delineation created by the connecting lead strips was respected. A few of the new churches were able to afford a complete set of their work – where the effect is awesome, if a little overpowering (examples can be seen at Brampton, Cumbria; Liverpool, All Hallows; and Selsey, Gloucestershire). Most churches could afford only one or two of their windows and it is from these places that the accompanying illustrations are taken.

COLOURS IN PAINTINGS

The wealthiest new churches could emulate the Middle Ages' tradition of covering all available wall space with painted or stencilled murals (see Chapter 6).

COLOURS IN FABRICS

Fabrics were only rarely used for tapestries, such as in wall coverings, as they required the most skilled and time-consuming work. However, highly decorated handmade fabrics could be used in altar frontals as well as High Church vestments, with much use of gold and silver threads and semi-precious stones.

Victorian traditions continued for a few years into the Edwardian era, most notably in the work of Ninian Comper (1864–1960). The years between the two World Wars and immediately after saw mainly a pale and diluted version of Victorian ideals. Since the 1960s, modern church people have created new and admired forms of building and furnishings in line with the contemporary spirit (see Chapter 19) but the religious and some of the artistic ideals of the Victorians still influence much of Christian worship today.

Liverpool, Tuebrook, St John the Baptist. As with Pugin's church at Cheadle, every available surface of G. F. Bodley's church of 1870 is brilliant with colour.
Opposite: The organ in the chancel.
Below: The tie-beam roof outmatches most of its medieval predecessors in bright colour.

Above: Bournemouth, St Peter, Dorset. A wealthy Anglo-Catholic vicar commissioned G. E. Street to build one of the great Victorian churches of England. As at Cheadle and Liverpool Tuebrook, every surface has coloured images.
Left: Paintings by G. F. Bodley, 1891, on the rib-vaulted chancel roof.
Right: Wall paintings on an arcade, 1907, follow a medieval tradition (see Chapter 6).

Hoarwithy, Herefordshire. The Byzantine-style dome mosaic above the altar shows Christ the Pantokrater against a background of gilded tessellae.

Above, left: Bywell, Northumberland. One of four chancel wall mosaics behind the altar, this one of St Andrew, church patron. They were part of the restoration of a Saxon church in the 1880s.

Above right and right: Ornate fabrics could contribute to the colour of an interior, usually in the form of altar frontals but occasionally as wall-hangings.
Above right: Brockhampton, Herefordshire. One of two tapestries used as an altar reredos, designed by Edward Burne-Jones and made by Morris and Co, 1901.
Right: Skelton, North Yorkshire. A section of the altar frontal made by the church benefactor Lady Mary Vyner of nearby Newby Hall in 1876.

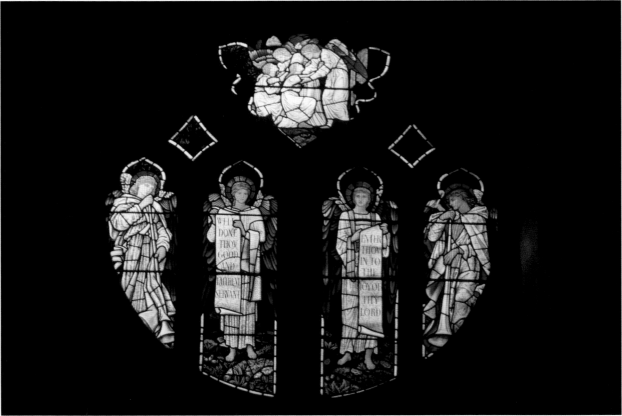

Four windows designed by Edward Burne-Jones and made by William Morris. The former painted in the pre-Raphaelite style, which aimed to eschew false grandeur in favour of naturalism. The latter was a founder of the Arts and Crafts movement, which turned away from mass-produced factory products in favour of handmade art, designed and made by one craftsman. Their work is characterised by richly glowing colours and clear designs, by far the best of the Victorian period.

Clockwise from top left:

Huish Episcopi, Somerset. Adoration of the Magi, 1899, a late work.

St Etheldreda's, Hatfield, Hertfordshire, 1894. Saints Martin and Margaret in the centre panels are flanked by angels. Small panels below show the corporal works of mercy; helping the thirsty, naked, sick and hungry.

Nun Monkton, West Yorkshire. St Ann and her daughter the Virgin Mary beneath an angel musician, 1873.

Brampton, Cumbria. A rose window with angel musicians, 1880.

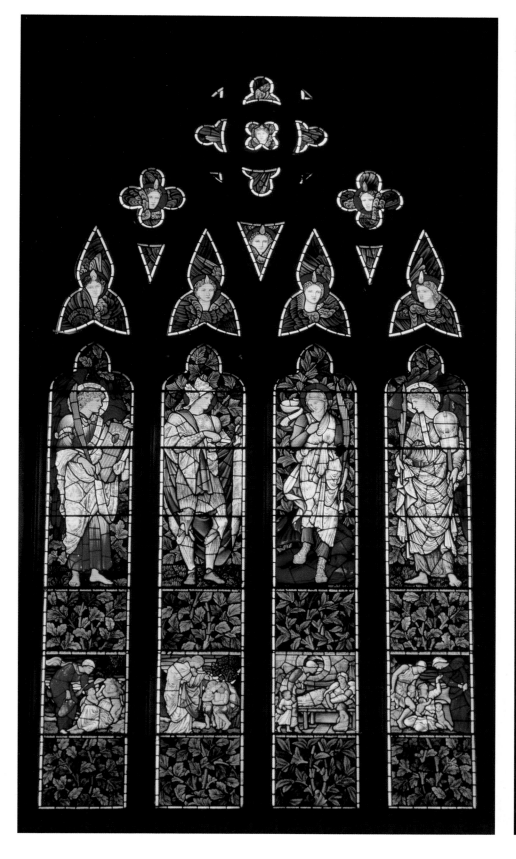

17
CURIOSITIES: ODDITIES AND BYGONES

THE ATTIC OF ANY HOUSE that the same family has occupied for a few generations may contain a variety of things discarded in the past. That is particularly true of an historical stately home owned by one family for hundreds of years. Here there are attics, lumber rooms and cellars holding forgotten things or items of sentimental value. Stables, workshops, barns and other estate buildings may be the resting places of old riding tackle, dog-carts, antique wheelchairs and agricultural implements from another age.

Churches are somewhat similar. In a few cases, clergy and parishioners have been reluctant to throw away venerable objects once of practical use but no longer needed. In addition, there are other things that are part of the fabric which may have seemed unexceptional at the time but now appear curious or even slightly disturbing. The following pages show a selection of diverse items which range over 1,800 years, presented in approximately chronological order.

The two oldest of the curiosities illustrated are from the Roman occupation of Britain.
Left: Wroxeter, Shropshire. The village is on the edge of the extensive remains of the second-century Roman town. Two columns from one of the buildings were erected as churchyard gates in the nineteenth century.
Right: Michaelchurch, Herefordshire. In this remote and lonely church there is a third-century Roman pillar-altar found nearby and placed here in 1830. A translation of the Latin inscription reads: 'To the God of Threeways (crossroads) Beccicus dedicates this altar...'

Rabbits appear occasionally – and endearingly – in medieval stonework.

Top: Barfreystone, Kent. Part of a Norman wall frieze shows a donkey and a monkey carrying a rabbit in a hod while a crouching man looks on.

Above: Elmley Castle, Worcestershire. A charmingly naïve fourteenth-century lone rabbit built into a wall inside the porch without a context – perhaps a reminder of dinner.

Right: Beverley St Mary, East Yorkshire. Early fourteenth-century carving of an upright-walking rabbit. He carries a satchel over his shoulder. Thought to be the model for John Tenniel's picture of the White Rabbit in Lewis Carroll's *Alice in Wonderland*. (See also the Long Melford window, Introduction, page 15, in which the Duchess is also thought to be a model for his illustrations.)

Two medieval chests, both amply padlocked to protect church plate and vestments.
Top: Lower Peover, Cheshire. A primitive thirteenth-century dug-out.
Bottom: Southwold, Suffolk. A much more sophisticated piece with St George fighting the dragon and much blank tracery.

Medieval misericords (the undersides of tip-up choir seats) display a famously eclectic range of carvings – religious, humorous, heraldic and satirical.
Top: Anstey, Hertfordshire. A woman puts out her tongue.
Bottom: Boston, St Botolph, Lincolnshire. A schoolmaster canes a schoolboy watched by others.

Top left: Bredon, Worcestershire. A fourteenth-century heart burial. People dying abroad, such as knights on campaign, were buried there but sometimes had their hearts repatriated to their parish church.

Above: Thefts of money from churches were probably as common in the Middle Ages, as today. At Blythborough, Suffolk, there is a strongly built example of a pillar poor-box designed for security in the fifteenth century.

Middle and bottom left: On medieval monuments it was common to place effigies of dogs, symbols of fidelity, at the feet of their masters or mistresses but stranger choices of animal occur.

Middle left: Framlingham, Suffolk. Henry Howard, Earl of Surrey, executed by Henry VIII in 1537 for treason has a boar at his feet.

Left: Wroxeter, Shropshire. Lord Chief Justice Bromley, died 1554, has a pheasant at his head.

Eighteenth-century aristocratic eccentricity and frivolity seldom exceed that seen in the font at West Wycombe, Buckinghamshire. The church was rebuilt by Sir Francis Dashwood, founder of the notorious Hellfire Club in 1750. The piece is made to resemble a garden birdbath, complete with doves drinking from the basin and another on the stem.

Above: Two examples of antique funeral equipment.
Left: Wingfield, Suffolk. A nineteenth-century graveside shelter for the parson in wet weather.
Right: Howden, East Yorkshire. A late seventeenth-century parish coffin on an eighteenth-century trolley (an early example of recycling).

Below: The twentieth century was occasionally capable of producing its own curiosities. At Fairford, Gloucestershire, Tibbles the church cat (1963–80) is commemorated outside the main entrance alongside many handsome eighteenth-century monuments in local Cotswold stone nearby.

18
THE NATION REMEMBERS THE WARS, 1900–1950

MEMORIES OF THE FIGHTING MEN in all manner of wars that took place between the thirteenth and nineteenth centuries were described in Chapter 11, but it seemed fitting to reserve a separate space for those killed in modern conflicts, many of them from generations still – just – within living memory. These memorials are more personal and heartfelt than those of distant wars, the causes and outcomes of which to many are only part of distantly remembered school history.

The twentieth century saw as many wars as any other and many more killed than in any other period.

Middleton, St Leonard, Greater Manchester. The memorial of 1903 for the Volunteer Yeomanry in the second Boer War shows soldiers with their packhorses and weapons.

The second Boer War between the British and Dutch Afrikaners in South Africa ended in 1902. The Great War of 1914–18, which was supposed to end all wars but did not, brought horrendous close-contact fighting in trenches in France and elsewhere, with huge loss of life by the bullet, the bayonet and poison gas. The various phases of the Second World War are more familiar. Since then Korea, Suez, the Gulf, Afghanistan, Northern Ireland and other places have seen British forces involved in conflict.

In their role as the most enduring buildings in the country, parish and cathedral churches have continued to be the preferred places to commemorate the fallen. From the end of the nineteenth century, monuments in stone or other materials have virtually disappeared. Stained glass has been the preferred medium, taking up no space and usually costing less, while still providing permanent and colourful reminders of brave sacrifices. The windows illustrated take us from the Boer War to the Second World War.

CHURCH MONUMENTS: AN EPILOGUE

In the late twentieth and early twenty-first centuries, a few families still wish to have memorials to their dead inside churches, mainly those who for centuries have installed great monuments in the same churches (see Chapter 10). A reticence entirely fitting to the present time, combined no doubt with financial considerations, has led to the appearance of small, dignified tablets usually of native slate or limestone with fine calligraphy and restrained wording. In their own way, they are as impressive and moving as any of the grandiosity of the past (see page 131).

Ingestre, Staffordshire. Monuments with effigies are extremely rare in the twentieth century. This splendid brass piece is of Viscount Captain Charles Alton Chetwynd-Taylor, who died during the First World War in 1915 aged 32 years. The fine seventeenth-century church is adjacent to his ancestral Ingestre Hall.

Glass for First World War military has its strongest expression of Christian piety when men are shown sharing the suffering of Christ.

Left: Shrewsbury, St Alkmund's. Christ is shown coming to a dying soldier.

Top: Brinsop, Herefordshire. Christ, centre is helped to carry His cross by a sailor left and a soldier, right. The badge of the Royal Flying Corps, the forerunner of the Royal Air Force is seen bottom centre.

Above: Mendlesham, Suffolk. A soldier is shown at the foot of the crucified Christ with Saints Michael and George on either side.

Memorial windows for First World War soldiers frequently link them to military saints and angels.
Left: Redgrave, Suffolk. The window for Captain the Hon Lyon Playfair, killed in action in 1915, shows Saints George, Michael the Archangel and Martin.
Right: Stokesay, Shropshire. The window for Lt Hotchkiss, killed in 1916, shows the idea of war leading to peace in the forms of Archangels Michael and Gabriel.

S·Michael Captain of the host   S·Gabriel Prince of Peace

City of London,
St Bartholomew's Hospital
Chapel. A memorial to
hundreds of nurses killed
on duty in the Second
World War.

LEAGUE OF ST BARTHOLOMEW'S NURSES

1939~1945

PRAISE GOD
REMEMBERING
THOSE NURSES FROM

THIS HOSPITAL WHO
GAVE THEIR LIVES
FOR THEIR
COUNTRY

AS BIRDS FLYING
SO SHALL THE LORD OF HOSTS PROTECT JERUSALEM

Above: Glass for the Second World War commemorates air force pilots as well as soldiers and sailors.
Above left: Durham Cathedral. Here the city recognises the work of the RAF in defending it against enemy bombers. A pilot rides on an eagle rising up to take to him to Archangel Michael with an apposite scriptural quotation below.
Above right: Great Underwood, Lincolnshire. The fighter and bomber squadrons of the United States Air Force operated from several airfields in the county and this recognises their role in the Second World War.

Below: Two restrained and dignified tablets commemorating greater and smaller landowners of the later twentieth century. In emotional impact they rival any of the larger and wordier monuments shown in earlier chapters.
Below left: Ashburnham, Sussex. To the last of a line in a parish church adjacent to a stately home deep inside its park.
Below right: Alton Priors, Wiltshire. For a man of the soil in a small, secluded church in fields at the edge of a village at the foot of the Marlborough Downs.

IN PERPETUAL MEMORY OF THE FAMILY OF ASHBURNHAM OF ASHBURNHAM WHO FOR MORE THAN EIGHT CENTURIES RULED AND SERVED THIS PLACE AND OF WHOM MANY LIE IN THE VAULT UNDER THIS CHAPEL AND IN SPECIAL AND PARTICULAR MEMORY OF LADY MARY CATHERINE ASHBURNHAM LAST OF THAT NAME AND LINE WHO DIED ON THE FIFTH DAY OF JANUARY 1953 AGED 63 AND LIES HERE WITH HER ANCESTORS MAY SHE AND THEY REST IN PEACE

20 July 1898 – 30 November 1978
ARTHUR GUY STRATTON
Farmed this land for sixty years

Canterbury Cathedral. *Peace*, 1956, by Ervin Bossanyi (1891–1976). A large window in which Christ, centre, towers over the whole picture, embracing children of several nations and races. The face of Christ shows power, love and grief. The Hungarian artist suffered in the two World Wars and this was a call to reconciliation in a city badly damaged by bombing. An early example of modern glass.

19
MODERN ART

Stained Glass, Paintings and Tapestries

Bristol, St Mary Redcliffe. *Madonna and Child* in the Lady Chapel, 1960, by Harry Stammers (1902–1962). They are surrounded by St John the Baptist, Eve and modern people. At this time Stammers used stylised natural forms.

THE PERIOD BETWEEN THE OUTBREAK of the First World War and the end of the Second World War saw little in the way of church building or furnishing. There was small need, given that there were more than enough such spaces already available, church people were preoccupied with more pressing concerns and that there was little money available. Whereas the Victorians had in many places revived the Gothic ethos with conviction in their own innovative interpretations, any work done now was largely a pale, worn-out imitation of Gothic with only an occasional glimpse of modern movements coming from mainland Europe.

Things started to change significantly in the 1940s. A leader in introducing modern works of art into churches was the Reverend Walter Hussey (1909–1985). As early as 1943 as Vicar of St Matthew's church, Northampton, he commissioned Henry Moore to make his now famous *Madonna and Child* and shortly afterwards commissioned a painting by Graham Sutherland. As Dean of Chichester from 1955, he commissioned Marc Chagall for glass, John Piper for tapestry and a number of other artists, as well as sacred music from Benjamin Britten, Lennox Berkeley, Malcolm Arnold and Leonard Bernstein. The trickle of similar activity that followed Hussey in other cathedrals and parish churches has now grown to a flood, just as it was in the Middle Ages. The works shown here are stained glass, paintings and tapestries which represent only a very small fraction of the whole.

Understandably, stained glass has played a predominant role in this movement. It can be installed easily in existing window space where there is clear glass or unsatisfactory older glass

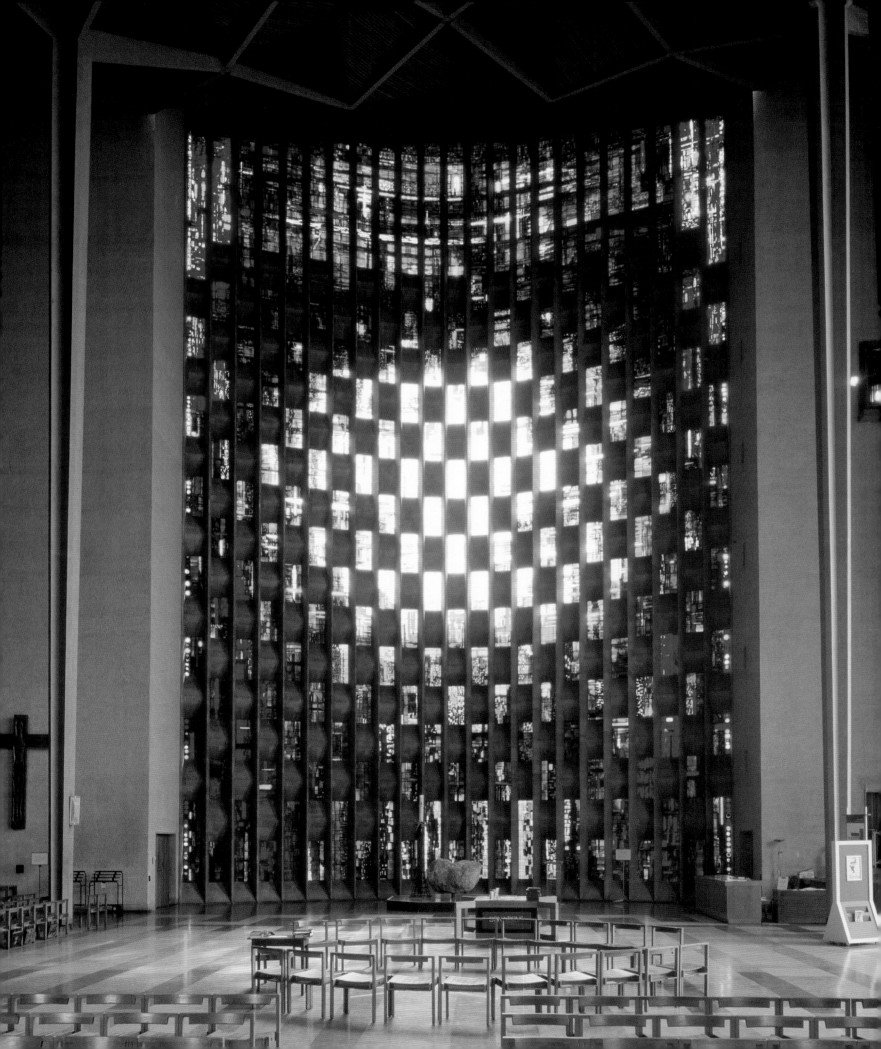

(one churchman in the City of London commented that if Second World War bomb damage done to the City churches had any good result it was that a large amount of poor Victorian glass had been destroyed). Smaller or larger windows can be chosen depending on the funds available, and the effects produced can be dramatic in providing new light and images in prominent or more private areas. Cathedrals and minster churches and the City of London churches mentioned above can call on financial patrons to commission leading glaziers, but thousands of ordinary parish churches that are financed solely by their congregations have been able to employ competent regional glaziers for excellent work (such as in the *dalle de verre* technique). In modern stained glass, dreary colours have disappeared and have been replaced by the rich glowing hues of the thirteenth century (see Chapter 3) and the Arts and Crafts (Chapter 16). Cliched iconography of static, insipid and often unrecognisable saints has been replaced by images with which the modern generation can identify. The abstract imagery widely seen in contemporary secular work has entered the churches and produced some attractive effects.

Paintings, ceramics and tapestries have been less widely commissioned, but the latter in particular have created vivid colour in otherwise sombre interiors. On the other hand, paintings that express the deeply felt faith and insights of the artist can convey spiritual understanding and inspiration to the viewers – just as they have done for centuries.

Contemporary art in whatever medium gives churches ancient and modern a feeling of being part of the present time and of being comfortable in it.

Coventry Cathedral. Abstract compositions in the nave, 1960, by Lawrence Lee (1909–2011), Geoffrey Clarke (1924–2014) and Keith New (1926–2012). **From top left clockwise**, they represent the transition from the chaos of the present world to the harmony of the Divine.

The extensive bombing of the City of London in the Second World War required much major rebuilding of Christopher Wren's damaged churches and this provided the opportunity to commission much new stained glass. Situated among the headquarters of many of the major financial organisations of the United Kingdom, it was possible to obtain the finance necessary to employ the leading glass artists of the day. Most of these combined clear modern styles with recognisable figurative iconography related to the particular church. All of these are by John Hayward, 1929–2007.

Above: St Mary-le-Bow, 1964. The Virgin Mary holds a model of the church and is surrounded by other City churches.

Top right: St Mary-le-Bow. St Thomas Becket who was born in the parish is at the top with the church steeple below.

Right: St Michael Paternoster Royal, 1968. A young Dick Whittington arrives in the City with his cat. He became Lord Mayor in 1397 and lived in the parish.

Top left: Leyland, St Mary Roman Catholic, Lancashire. Abstract composition by Patrick Reyntiens, 1967. The central nave and chancel areas of the building are surrounded internally by a circular ambulatory divided into bays by concrete supports. Each bay is filled with small irregularly shaped pieces of glass set into concrete with resin, the *dalle de verre* technique being 'very pretty in colour and shape'. The church is staffed by Benedictine monks of an order long familiar with architectural innovation.

Top right: Many ordinary parish churches with limited finances are able to commission works from skilled regional glaziers. This one at Bunbury, Cheshire is a Crucifixion with ministering angels by Ann Sotheran, 2005.

Left and opposite: Two compositions by Alan Younger (1933–2004) in different styles, abstract and figurative, but using the same attractive combination of colours.

Left: Enville, Staffordshire. A Madonna and Child with side figures, 2000, to celebrate the millennium.

Opposite: Chester Cathedral. One of three adjacent windows to celebrate the 9th centenary of the cathedral in 2000. They were donated by the Duke of Westminster of nearby Eaton Hall.

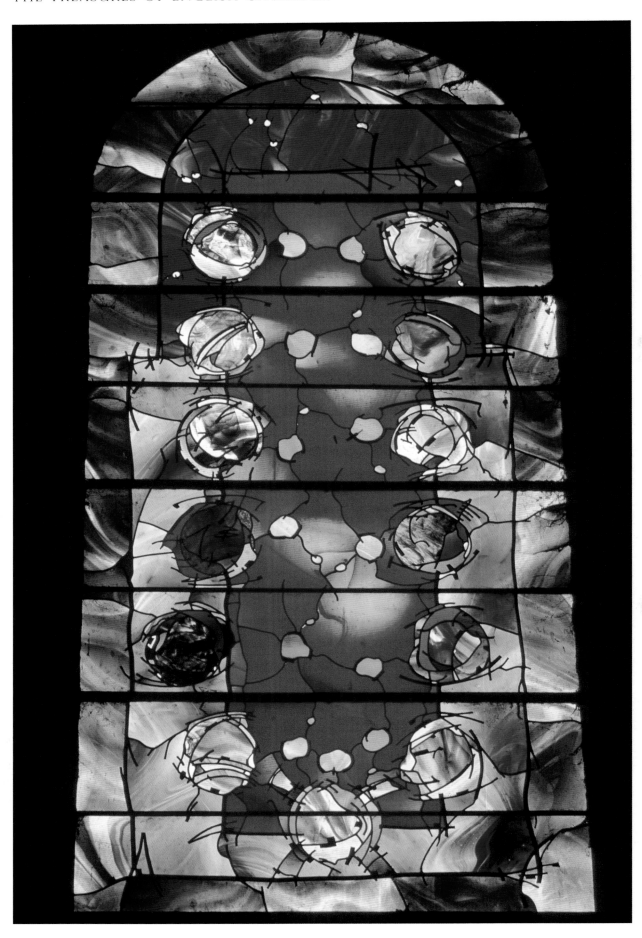

Opposite: Hereford Cathedral. One of four windows in the tiny cell-like chantry chapel of Bishop Audley, 2007, by Tom Denny (b.1964). They celebrate the life of Thomas Traherne, a Herefordshire priest, 1637–1674, whose spirituality and writings exulted in God's natural world. This window shows a tree-lined pool below fed by a spring. Above this a tiny figure runs into the distance through a cornfield. These windows are among the most beautiful and interesting modern glass in England, as are others by Denny in Gloucester Cathedral and elsewhere.

Left: Durham Cathedral. *The Bread of Life*, 1984, by Mark Angus (b.1949). The work stands out as markedly different in style from any of the windows shown but similar to that of David Hockney and others. It is an 'aerial' view of the Last Supper with Christ and the twelve Apostles. Judas is identified as sitting out of line from the others. It was donated by employees of the Durham branch of Marks and Spencer to mark the centenary of the firm.

Northampton, St Matthew. *A Crucifixion*, 1948, by Graham Sutherland (1903–1980). Pevsner describes how this work was inspired by Mathis Grünewald's Crucifixion of 1515 at Isenheim Abbey in Germany. The abbey had a plague hospital and the tormented figure of Christ placed within sight of the victims was intended to inspire faith and hope.

Liverpool Anglican Cathedral. *The Good Samaritan*, 1991, by Adrian Wiszniewski (b.1958). At first sight this painting, prominently displayed in the chancel, could not be more different from Sutherland's Crucifixion, opposite. In fact both depict suffering, albeit of a different kind in a very different place at very different times. The painting is a modern take on the New Testament parable of the Good Samaritan (Luke 10:25–37). Here the victim of robbers is shown as a young man stripped naked with a knife and blood at his feet. The Good Samaritan is shown, unusually, as a woman offering him water while the indifferent passers-by take the form of young professionals exchanging business cards and a young woman gazing uncaringly into the distance. The commissioning of such a painting says something of the courage of modern clergy in using a tough modern city centre version of the Gospel (the cathedral borders the Toxteth area of Liverpool) to convey its message to the current generation.

Chichester Cathedral. This tapestry of 1966 by John Piper, which hangs as a reredos immediately behind the high altar, brings bright colours to a rather dark area of the cathedral. At the centre of the composition, within a triangular area, there are the symbols of the Holy Trinity: an orb for the Father, a 'tau' cross for the Son and flames for the Holy Spirit. The side panels contain symbols of created life – animals, fishes and plants. The symbols of the Evangelists are at the base. The work and its positioning has inevitably attracted both praise and criticism.

Chichester Cathedral. This tapestry installed in 1983 hangs in the restored shrine of St Richard (Bishop of Chichester 1245–53) which is back to back with the high altar reredos and Piper tapestry above. It was designed and made by German and English artists in a spirit of reconciliation between the two nations after the Second World War and as a memorial to Bishop George Bell of Chichester who strove for reconciliation during and after the war. A large 'chalice' shape and a cross within represent St Richard. A variety of other symbols include a dove for the Holy Spirit, a serpent for evil and temptation, and a lotus for birth and life.

These two late twentieth-century pieces of art surrounded by twelfth-century architecture are typical of the way in which Christian churches continuously marry the ancient and the modern, a consistent theme of this book.

ACKNOWLEDGEMENTS
AND FURTHER READING

PEVSNER, NIKOLAUS. THE COUNTY VOLUMES of his *Buildings of England* series were first published 1951–74 and have now been extensively enlarged and revised by other writers. Pevsner was one of the most scholarly and widely travelled of architectural historians, visiting and recording almost every building of architectural interest — ecclesiastical, domestic, public and industrial — in the cities, towns, villages and hamlets of England. These include tens of thousands of churches and chapels, in which exteriors, interiors and furnishings are described in a concise and readable style. These books are indispensable travelling companions for all church explorers. They have guided me in my own travels and have provided much of the factual data in this book. Unless otherwise stated, all direct quotations are from this source. The most recent editions are published by Yale University Press.

Betjeman's Best British Churches. John Betjeman's original classic guide has now been updated and enlarged by Richard Surman. Collins, 2011. It contains comprehensive lists of the best churches in each county, from the interesting to the outstanding.

Clifton-Taylor, Alex. *English Parish Churches as Works of Art*. Batsford, 1974. Another well-travelled writer whose immense enthusiasm for his subject permeates his book, which includes an appendix listing the very finest churches in each county.

Friar, Stephen. *The Companion Guide to the English Parish Church*. Chancellor Press, 2000. An A-to-Z encyclopaedia of church history, church personalities, architecture and furniture, down to the smallest details.

Jones, Lawrence E. *The Beauty of English Churches*. Constable, 1978. A concise mini encyclopaedia of church buildings and furnishings, with several gazetteers to each subject area.

To these must be added the thousands of informative guides published by individual parishes, ranging from one-sheet leaflets to substantial illustrated booklets. They are a particularly valuable source of local details.

HOW TO SUPPORT THE NATIONAL CHURCHES TRUST

Many of the UK's historic churches are fighting a battle against the ravages of time.

We need to make sure they get the help they need to remain open and at the heart of the local communities for which they were built and so continue to play an integral part in all our lives.

The National Churches Trust (formerly the Historic Churches Preservation Trust) relies on the generosity of our supporters to fund our work. In 2020 we awarded grants to over 220 churches, chapels and meeting houses and we supported many, many more. People choose to help us in different ways:

BECOME A FRIEND

Thanks to the help of our Friends, we are able to fund urgent repairs to thousands of churches across the UK. By joining us today, you can help us to do even more. Not only will your support make a vital difference to our work, but you will also enjoy a range of benefits.

For more information and to join online visit www.nationalchurchestrust.org/friends

LEAVE A GIFT IN YOUR WILL

By leaving a gift in your Will to the National Churches Trust you can help us restore churches in every sense of the word. A gift of just 1% of your estate will help to guarantee that our nation's rich heritage of churches and chapels will survive for many years to come.

If you would like more information on leaving a gift in your will or adding a codicil, please visit our website www.nationalchurchestrust.org/legacy, or contact us on 020 7222 0605 or email Claire Walker, Chief Executive, at claire.walker@nationalchurchestrust.org — there is no obligation and we would be delighted to help you further.

MAKE A DONATION

You can make a donation online at www.nationalchurchestrust.org/donate

Our churches, chapels and meeting houses are a unique part of our national story. With your help we can do more to ensure their survival for the benefit of future generations.

Thank you.

CONTACT US AT:

The National Churches Trust,
7 Tufton Street,
London SW1P 3QB
020 7222 0605
info@nationalchurchestrust.org
www.nationalchurchestrust.org
Registered Charity Number 1119845

Huw Edwards, Bill Bryson, Michael Palin and Joe Stilgoe at the National Churches Trust's 2019 Carol Concert at St James's church, Piccadilly.
© Andy Sillett

INDEX

References to images are in *italics*.